The Sainsbury Book of
INDIAN COOKING
Naomi Good

CONTENTS

Published exclusively for
J Sainsbury plc
Stamford Street, London SE1 9LL
by Cathay Books
59 Grosvenor Street, London W1

First published 1984
Reprinted 1985

© Cathay Books 1984

ISBN 0 86178 254 2

Printed in Hong Kong

NOTES

Standard spoon measurements are
used in all recipes.
1 tablespoon = one 15 ml spoon
1 teaspoon = one 5 ml spoon
All spoon measures are level.

Use freshly ground black pepper
where pepper is specified.
Use whole black peppercorns
where peppercorns are specified.

Ovens should be preheated to the
specified temperature.

For all recipes, quantities are given
in both metric and imperial
measures. Follow either set but not
a mixture of both, because they are
not interchangeable.

Ingredients marked with an
asterisk are explained on
pages 8 to 11.

INTRODUCTION

The splendid thing about Indian cooking is that most of the recipes can be prepared in advance and the dishes then heated just before serving without coming to any harm.

A simple methodical approach to preparing Indian food also makes entertaining easier. Assemble all the ingredients needed for the recipe before you begin to cook. Measure out all the spices and seasonings and put them on a plate in separate piles. Chop, slice, grate or process fresh ingredients and have them ready on your board. The recipe will then be very simple to follow with everything to hand.

A traditional Indian family meal usually consists of one meat, poultry or fish dish, one vegetable dish, and one lentil dish, served with rice or bread and accompanied by yogurt, and chutneys or pickles. Desserts are not usually served for everyday meals.

When entertaining, an extra meat or fish dish and an additional vegetable dish will be served and the meal ended with a dessert or a selection of sweetmeats.

It is important that the chosen dishes contrast with each other in colour, texture and flavour. This balance makes the meal attractive to both the eye and the palate and gives the meal its typical Indian zest.

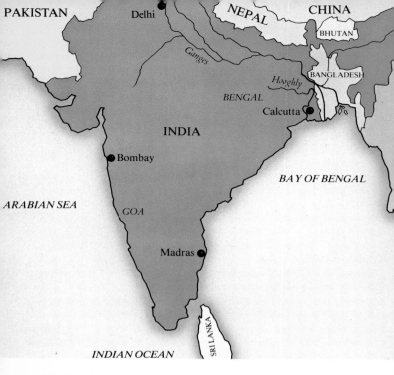

REGIONAL COOKING

India is a large country with many regional variations in climate, custom, religion and food. The country has been invaded and colonized many times, and each time changes have taken place in the eating habits of the local population.

When the Moguls descended on northern India in the sixteenth century they brought with them their rich meat-based cuisine. From central Asia, too, came the *tandoor*, the clay oven, which gives its name to those delectable dishes now served in every Indian restaurant.

The north is a wheat-growing, bread-eating area. The preferred cooking fat is ghee*, although substitutes are used. Generally speaking the food is mild; it gets progressively hotter and spicier the farther south you go.

The population of India is predominantly Hindu and vegetarian. When Hindus eat meat it is usually lamb – never beef, for the cow is sacred. There are, of course, many meat-eating minorities: the Goans from the ex-Portuguese colony on the west coast for whom pork is a speciality; the Muslims who eat beef and lamb but never pork; the Parsees who are omnivorous.

The more southern states grow rice as their staple food, use oil in preference to ghee and tend to be vegetarian. In Bengal on the east coast the food is again different, as they

6

have plenty of fish – especially plump king-size prawns and lobsters – in the tidal waters of the Hooghly river. Mustard seeds and mustard oil are popular here too. But best of all are their sweets – little white and brown spheres floating in syrup and fudge-like pink, white and green squares.

All Indians love sweets but leave the making of them to the professionals. Those sweets that are simple enough to be made at home require patience rather than skill and the full attention of the cook or the results will be disappointing.

EQUIPMENT
In India the traditional method of grinding spices to a paste or powder is in a large mortar or on a flat stone using a heavy rolling-pin shaped stone. Here an electric blender with a strong motor or a food processor will make quick work of puréeing spices.

To grind small quantities of dry spices a coffee grinder is ideal – but you will not be able to use it for grinding coffee again. If you do not have a blender, a mezzaluna (a curved blade with two handles), a garlic press and a grater will give very satisfactory results.

In India saucepans do not have handles. They used to be made of heavy copper with tinned interiors and curved bottoms, but now they are often made from aluminium and are flat bottomed.

For frying, a large heavy wok-like pan is used and for making bread a slightly curved, iron plate-like griddle. Any heavy frying pan can be used instead.

In a traditional Indian household plates are not used. Instead they serve food on *thalis*, round trays made from metal, usually brass although stainless steel is becoming more commonly used especially in urban areas, and silver (by those who can afford it) for special occasions. Small bowls called *katoris* are placed on the tray and filled with the various dishes. Chutneys and accompaniments are arranged on the *thali* itself as are breads such as puris or chapatis. Rice is also served directly on to the tray. In the south banana leaves are sometimes used and make delightful disposable *thalis*.

At the end of a meal, especially if it has been a heavy one, *paan* is served as a *digestif* and an astringent mouth freshener. *Paan* is made from the leaf of the betel palm, spread with lime (calcium) paste and filled with chopped betel nut and a variety of spices such as cloves, cardamom seeds and aniseed. The leaf is then neatly folded into a triangle small enough to be popped whole into the mouth. It turns the mouth red when chewed and is addictive especially when the ingredients include tobacco.

SPECIALIST INGREDIENTS

The following are available from Asian food stores and other specialist shops, some supermarkets, delicatessens and greengrocers:

Cardamom (elaichi) An aromatic seed pod which comes in three varieties: white, green (more perfumed than the white) and large black (not always available). The whole pod is used to flavour rice and meat dishes and then discarded, or the pod is opened and the seeds removed and crushed for sprinkling on sweets or vegetables.

Cayenne pepper or chilli powder Powdered dried red chillies. The strength varies from batch to batch. Use with caution.

Chillies, hot fresh green (hari mirch) Use with care. For a less pungent result slit the chillies and discard the seeds. Do not touch your face or rub your eyes while handling chillies, and wash your hands immediately afterwards.

Chillies, dried red (sabat lal mirch) These add a good flavour when tossed in whole with other frying spices. The smaller ones are very pungent so add them cautiously. They can also be crumbled between finger tips, if preferred. Handle with the same care as green chillies (above).

Cinnamon (dalchini) Available in stick and ground form. The stick should be discarded before the dish is served.

Coconut (narial) Used in many sweet and savoury dishes. When buying a coconut choose one that is heavy for its size. To open it, pierce the 'eyes' with a skewer and pour away the liquid. Put the coconut in a preheated moderately hot oven, 190°C (375°F), Gas Mark 5, for 15 minutes, then place on a sturdy table or on the floor and give it a sharp tap with a mallet or hammer; it will break in two. Using a sharp knife, prise away the flesh from the shell, then peel off the brown skin and cut the coconut into pieces.

If the coconut is already open – Indian shopkeepers will do it for you – put it in the oven for 15 to 20 minutes or until you hear the shell cracking. The flesh will then be easy to remove.

Grate the coconut in a food processor or by hand and use as required.

Coconut milk is an infusion used to flavour and thicken many dishes, particularly in Southern India. To make coconut milk, place the grated coconut in a bowl, pour over about 600 ml (1 pint) boiling water, just to cover and leave for 1 hour. Strain through muslin, squeezing hard to extract as much 'milk' as possible. This is called 'thick' coconut milk. To make 'thin' coconut milk pour another 600 ml (1 pint) of boiling water over the coconut flesh from which the thick milk has already been extracted, and repeat the process.

Bought creamed coconut is a very useful substitute.

Coriander, fresh green (hara dhanya) A delicate, fragrant herb. Used chopped to sprinkle over dishes as a garnish or stirred in at the end of the cooking time or puréed to make sauces and chutneys. Parsley may be substituted, but it doesn't have the same flavour.

Coriander seeds (dhanya) Come whole or ground. Used a lot in ground form. Very fragrant.

Cumin seeds (zeera) There are many varieties of this strong flavoured, caraway-like seed. The black variety is best. Comes ground or whole.

Curry leaves (kari patta) Aromatic leaves of the sweet Nim tree, available dried. They release a very appetizing smell when cooked.

Fennel seeds (sonf) These aniseed-flavoured seeds are often chewed as a digestive. They add a fine flavour and aroma to many dishes.

Garam Masala A ground spice mixture used in many recipes. You can buy it or prepare your own: the flavour is obviously better when it is freshly ground. To make garam masala, place 2 tablespoons black peppercorns, 1 tablespoon black cumin seeds, 1 small cinnamon stick, 1 teaspoon whole cloves, ¼ nutmeg, 2 teaspoons cardamom seeds and 2 tablespoons coriander seeds in a coffee grinder and grind to a powder. Store in a screw-topped jar.

Ghee (clarified butter) A good cooking fat. It is better than butter because it can be heated to a higher temperature without burning. Ghee can be bought in tins or made at home. To make ghee, place 250 g (8 oz) unsalted butter in a small pan over low heat. Bring to just below simmering point and cook for 20 to 30 minutes or until it has stopped sputtering and is beginning to change colour. Strain through several thicknesses of muslin. Keep in a screw-topped jar in a cool place – refrigeration is not necessary.

250 g (8 oz) butter makes 175-200 ml (6-7 fl oz) ghee. Larger quantities take a little longer to make.

Ginger, fresh (adrak) A khaki-coloured, knobbly rhizome. Should be smooth and fresh looking. Keep in a plastic bag in the refrigerator. Always peel before using. It can be grated, finely chopped or puréed in an electric blender or food processor.

Ginger, dried (sonth) Sold whole or powdered. Does not give as good a flavour as fresh ginger.

Gram flour (bessan) Ground chick peas or split peas. Excellent for making batter and used in place of flour.

Mustard seeds (sarson) Small, round reddish-black seeds. When fried for a few seconds they sputter with the heat and give out a delicious smell.

Oil Use any vegetable oil for cooking Indian food. Ground nut oil is commonly used in India.

Panir (Indian cheese) A curd cheese used in cooking. To make panir, bring 1.2 litres (2 pints) milk to the boil, remove from heat and stir in a bare ¼ teaspoon tartaric acid dissolved in 120 ml (4 fl oz) hot water. Stir gently until the milk curdles, then leave for 30 minutes. Line a sieve with muslin and strain the curdled milk, squeezing out all the liquid. Form the remaining curds into a rough rectangle about 1-1.5 cm (½-¾ inch) deep in the same cloth and wrap it tightly round. Place this packet between two flat surfaces and place a 2.5 kg (5 lb) weight on top. Leave for 2 to 3 hours. 1.2 litres (2 pints) milk makes 125 g (4 oz) panir.

Pulses (dhals) These form an important part of the Indian diet. There are nearly 60 varieties in India but the most commonly used are mung, both olive green and yellow; *masoor* or Egyptian lentils – the common salmon pink lentils available in every supermarket; *channa* – split peas; *kabli channa* or Bengal gram – whole peas; *tur* – the vari-coloured pigeon-pea; *lobia* – black-eyed peas; and *rajma* – red kidney beans.

Saffron (kesar) Available in threads and in powdered form. The threads are soaked in hot water or milk before using. Saffron gives food a lovely yellow colour and a fine aroma and taste. Expensive but worth it.

Sesame seeds (til) These have a fine nutty flavour. They are used to flavour some vegetable dishes and to sprinkle on *naan*.

Tamarind (imli) Pods from the tamarind tree, used as a souring agent. Sold as pods or pulp – pulp is easier to use. Both must be soaked in hot water, then squeezed and strained before use. Vinegar or lemon juice may be used instead.

Turmeric (haldi) A rhizome commonly used in its powdered form for its earthy taste and yellow colour. It stains clothing and work surfaces so be careful not to spill it.

Yogurt (dhai) Yogurt is eaten daily all over India, either plain or with vegetables or fruit mixed in. It is also used in cooking, particularly in the north. Yogurt is quite easy to make at home, using a special machine or electric oven.

To make yogurt, bring 600 ml (1 pint) milk to the boil. As the milk begins to rise in the pan, take it off the heat and dip the pan in cold water to cool. Put 2 teaspoons bought natural yogurt in a heatproof bowl and stir well. Pour over the warm milk and mix well. Place in a preheated very cool oven – as low as your oven will go – and cook for 30 minutes. Turn off the heat and leave the bowl in the oven for 5 hours or until the yogurt is set, switching the heat on and off as necessary during this time to maintain the temperature.

SAVOURIES

Ekuri

50 g (2 oz) butter
1 onion, finely
   chopped
2 green chillies*,
   finely chopped
8 eggs, lightly beaten
   with 2 tablespoons
   water
1 tablespoon finely
   chopped coriander*
salt

Heat the butter in a pan, add the
onion and fry until deep golden. Add
the chillies and fry for 30 seconds,
then add the eggs, coriander and salt
to taste, and cook, stirring, until the
eggs are scrambled and set. Serve hot.
Serves 4

Shish Kebab

500 g (1 lb) minced
  lamb
2 tablespoons finely
  chopped celery
  leaves
2 tablespoons
  chopped parsley
2 onions, finely
  chopped
1 teaspoon turmeric*
salt and pepper
TO GARNISH:
chopped parsley
finely chopped onion

Mix all the ingredients together very
thoroughly, seasoning with salt and
pepper to taste. Roll the mixture into
thin sausage shapes and cook under a
preheated moderate grill for about 10
minutes, turning several times. Serve
garnished with parsley and chopped
onion.
Serves 4

Pakora

125 g (4 oz) gram
   flour*
1 teaspoon salt
½ teaspoon chilli
   powder*
about 150 ml (¼
   pint) water
2 green chillies*,
   finely chopped
1 tablespoon finely
   chopped coriander*
1 teaspoon melted
   butter or ghee*
2 onions, cut into
   rings
oil for deep-frying
8 small fresh spinach
   leaves
2-3 potatoes, par-
   boiled and sliced

Sift the flour, salt and chilli powder into a bowl. Stir in sufficient water to make a thick batter and beat well until smooth. Leave to stand for 30 minutes.

Stir the chillies and coriander into the batter, then add the melted butter or ghee. Drop in the onion rings to coat thickly with batter.

Heat the oil in a deep pan, drop in the onion rings and deep-fry until crisp and golden. Remove from the pan with a slotted spoon, drain on kitchen paper and keep warm.

Dip the spinach leaves into the batter and deep-fry in the same way, adding more oil to the pan if necessary.

Finally, repeat the process with the potato slices.

Serve hot.

Serves 4

Chicken Tikka

150 g (5.2 oz)
   natural yogurt
1 tablespoon grated
   ginger*
2 cloves garlic,
   crushed
1 teaspoon chilli
   powder*
1 tablespoon ground
   coriander seeds*
½ teaspoon salt
juice of 1 lemon
2 tablespoons oil
750 (1½ lb) chicken
   breasts, skinned
   and boned
TO GARNISH:
1 onion, sliced
2 tomatoes, quartered
4 lemon twists

Mix together in a bowl all the ingredients except the chicken. Cut the chicken into cubes and drop into the marinade. Cover and leave in the refrigerator overnight.

Thread the chicken on to 4 skewers and cook under a preheated hot grill for 5 to 6 minutes, turning frequently.

Remove the chicken from the skewers and arrange on individual serving plates. Garnish with onion, tomato and lemon to serve.

Serves 4

Meat Samosa

PASTRY:
125 g (4 oz) plain
  flour
1/4 teaspoon salt
25 g (1 oz) ghee* or
  butter
2-3 tablespoons water

FILLING:
1 tablespoon oil
1 small onion, minced
1 clove garlic, crushed
1 green chilli*,
  minced
1/2 teaspoon chilli
  powder*
250 g (8 oz) minced
  beef
125 g (4 oz) tomato,
  skinned and
  chopped
1 tablespoon chopped
  coriander*
salt

oil for deep-frying

Sift the flour and salt into a mixing bowl. Rub in the ghee or butter until the mixture resembles breadcrumbs. Add the water and knead thoroughly to a very smooth dough. Cover and chill while preparing the filling.

Heat the oil in a pan, add the onion and garlic and fry until golden. Add the chilli and chilli powder and fry for 3 minutes. Stir in the meat and cook until well browned. Add the tomato, coriander, and salt to taste and simmer gently for 20 minutes, until the meat is tender and the mixture is dry; skim off any fat. Stir well and cool slightly.

Divide the pastry into 8 pieces. Dust with flour and roll each piece into a thin round, then cut each round in half. Fold each half into a cone and brush the seam with water to seal.

Fill the cone with a spoonful of filling (do not overfill), dampen the top edge and seal firmly. Deep-fry until crisp and golden. Serve hot or warm.
Serves 4

Vegetable Samosa

PASTRY:
125 g (4 oz) plain flour
¼ teaspoon salt
25 g (1 oz) ghee* or butter
2-3 tablespoons water

FILLING:
1 tablespoon oil
1 teaspoon mustard seeds*
1 small onion, minced
2 green chillies*, minced
¼ teaspoon turmeric*
1 teaspoon finely chopped ginger*
salt
125 g (4 oz) frozen peas
125 g (4 oz) cooked potatoes, diced
½ tablespoon chopped coriander*
1 tablespoon lemon juice
oil for deep-frying

Make the pastry as for Meat Samosa (opposite). Chill while preparing the filling.

Heat the oil in a pan and add the mustard seeds. Leave for a few seconds until they start to pop, then add the onion and fry until golden. Add the chillies, turmeric, ginger, and salt to taste and fry for 3 minutes; if it starts sticking to the pan add ½ tablespoon water and stir well. Add the peas, stir well and cook for 2 minutes. Add the potatoes and coriander, stir well and cook for 1 minute. Stir in the lemon juice. Cool slightly.

Shape and cook as for Meat Samosa. Serve hot or warm.

Serves 4

MEAT DISHES

Meat Puffs

3 tablespoons self-
   raising flour
3 eggs, beaten
5-6 tablespoons water
250 g (8 oz) minced
   beef
1 bunch of spring
   onions, finely
   sliced
1 green chilli*, finely
   chopped
1 teaspoon turmeric*
salt
oil for frying

Sift the flour into a bowl, add the eggs and beat well to combine. Gradually add enough water to make a thick creamy batter, beating well.

Stir in the minced beef, onions, chilli, turmeric, and salt to taste; the mixture should be like a stiff porridge. Leave in a warm place for 1 hour.

Heat about 1 cm (½ inch) depth of oil in a frying pan. When really hot, drop in spoonfuls of the meat mixture and fry on each side for 2 minutes. Drain well and keep warm while cooking the remainder, adding more oil as required. Serve hot.

Serves 4

Brinjal Cutlets

2 large aubergines
salt
3 tablespoons oil
1 onion, finely
    chopped
1 clove garlic, finely
    chopped
2 green chillies*,
    seeded and finely
    chopped
1 teaspoon turmeric*
500 g (1 lb) minced
    beef
1 egg, lightly beaten
2-3 tablespoons fresh
    breadcrumbs

Cook the aubergines in boiling salted water for 15 minutes or until almost tender. Drain thoroughly and cool.

Heat the oil in a pan, add the onion and fry until golden. Add the garlic, chillies and turmeric and fry for 2 minutes. Add the mince and cook, stirring, until brown all over. Add salt to taste and cook gently for 20 minutes, until the meat is tender.

Cut the aubergines in half lengthways. Carefully scoop out the pulp, add it to the meat mixture and mix well. Check the seasoning. Fill the aubergine shells with the mixture, brush with egg and cover with breadcrumbs. Cook under a preheated moderate grill for 4 to 5 minutes, until golden.

Serves 4

Kheema with Potatoes and Peas

4 tablespoons oil
2 onions, finely
  chopped
2 teaspoons ground
  coriander seeds*
½ teaspoon ground
  cumin seeds*
½ teaspoon ground
  turmeric*
2.5 cm (1 inch) piece
  ginger*, finely
  chopped
1 chilli*, finely
  chopped
1 heaped teaspoon
  garam masala*
500 g (1 lb) minced
  beef
250 g (8 oz) small
  potatoes, quartered
salt
500 g (1 lb) shelled
  peas

Heat the oil in a lidded frying pan,
add the onions and cook until soft.
Add the spices and fry for 5 minutes
over low heat; add 1 tablespoon water
if the mixture starts to burn. Stir in
the minced beef and cook over high
heat until very well browned.

Lower the heat and add the
potatoes and salt to taste. Cover and
cook gently for 5 minutes, then add
the peas. Continue cooking until the
potatoes and peas are tender. Serve
hot.
Serves 4

Kofta in Yogurt

500 g (1 lb) minced
  beef
75 g (3 oz) fresh
  breadcrumbs
2 green chillies*,
  finely chopped
1 onion, finely
  chopped
2.5 cm (1 inch) piece
  ginger*, finely
  chopped
2 teaspoons ground
  coriander seeds*
salt
1 egg, lightly beaten
oil for frying
500 g (1 lb) natural
  yogurt
2 tablespoons finely
  chopped coriander*

Mix the minced beef, breadcrumbs,
chillies, onion, ginger, ground
coriander, salt to taste and egg
together and shape the mixture into
walnut-sized balls.

Heat the oil in a large pan, add the
meat balls and fry until well browned
and cooked through. Drain carefully.

Pour the yogurt into a serving
bowl and add the meat balls while
still hot. Sprinkle with the chopped
coriander and serve warm.
Serves 4

Chilli Fry

4 tablespoons oil
1 large onion, finely
    chopped
1/2 teaspoon ground
    coriander seeds*
1/2 teaspoon turmeric*
2.5 cm (1 inch) piece
    ginger*, finely
    chopped
1 chilli*, chopped
500 g (1 lb) frying
    steak, cut into
    strips about 2.5 ×
    1 cm (1 × 1½ inch)
1 green or red pepper,
    cored, seeded and
    roughly chopped
2 tomatoes, quartered
juice of 1 lemon
salt

Heat the oil in a lidded frying pan, add
the onion and fry until soft. Add the
coriander, turmeric, ginger and chilli
and fry over low heat for 5 minutes;
if the mixture becomes dry, add
1 tablespoon water.

Add the steak, increase the heat
and cook, stirring, until browned all
over. Add the chopped pepper, cover
and simmer gently for 5 to 10 minutes,
until the meat is tender. Add the
tomatoes, lemon juice and salt to
taste and cook, uncovered, for 2 to
3 minutes.

Serves 4

NOTE: This dish should be rather dry.

Aloo 'Chops'

3 tablespoons oil
1 large onion, finely
  chopped
1 cm (½ inch) piece
  ginger*, finely
  chopped
1 teaspoon ground
  coriander seeds*
250 g (8 oz) minced
  beef
1 tablespoon raisins
salt
1 tablespoon finely
  chopped coriander*
1 kg (2 lb) potatoes,
  boiled and mashed
  with a little milk
  and salt
flour for coating
oil for shallow frying

Heat the oil in a frying pan, add the
onion and ginger and fry until
golden. Add the ground coriander
and minced beef and fry until brown.
Add the raisins and salt to taste and
simmer for about 20 minutes, until
the meat is cooked. Spoon out any fat
in the pan. Stir in the chopped
coriander and leave to cool.

Divide the mashed potato into
8 portions. With well floured hands,
flatten a portion on one palm, put
3 teaspoons of the meat mixture in
the centre and fold the potato over it.
Form gently into a round patty shape.

Dip the 'chops' lightly in flour and
shallow fry a few at a time in hot oil,
until crisp and golden, turning
carefully to brown the underside.
Serves 4

Stuffed Pimento

5 tablespoons oil
1 onion, finely
  chopped
2 teaspoons ground
  coriander seeds*
1 teaspoon ground
  cumin seeds*
½ teaspoon chilli
  powder*
350 g (12 oz) minced
  beef
3 tablespoons long-
  grain rice
salt
4 large green or red
  peppers
1 × 397 g (14 oz)
  can tomatoes

Heat 3 tablespoons of the oil in a
saucepan, add the onion and fry until
golden. Add the spices and cook for
2 minutes. Add the minced beef and
fry, stirring, until browned. Add the
rice and salt to taste and cook for
2 minutes. Remove from the heat
and leave to cool.
   Slice the peppers lengthways and
discard the seeds and cores. Fill the
pepper shells with the meat mixture.
   Heat the remaining oil in a pan just
large enough to hold the peppers.
Place the peppers in the pan. Pour a
little of the tomato juice into each
pepper and the remaining juice and
tomatoes into the pan, seasoning with
salt to taste. Bring to simmering
point, cover and cook for about
25 minutes, until the rice is tender.
Serves 4

Beef Curry with Potatoes

4 tablespoons oil
2 onions, finely
  chopped
2 cloves garlic,
  chopped
1 teaspoon chilli
  powder*
1 tablespoon ground
  cumin seeds*
1½ tablespoons
  ground coriander
  seeds*
2.5 cm (1 inch) piece
  ginger*, finely
  chopped
750 g (1½ lb)
  stewing steak, cubed
2 tablespoons tomato
  purée
salt
350 g (12 oz) new
  potatoes
4 green chillies*

Heat the oil in a large pan, add the onions and fry until lightly coloured. Add the garlic, chilli powder, cumin, coriander and ginger and cook gently for 5 minutes, stirring occasionally; if the mixture becomes dry, add 2 tablespoons water.

Add the beef and cook, stirring, until browned all over. Add the tomato purée, salt to taste and just enough water to cover the meat; stir very well. Bring to the boil, cover and simmer for about 1 hour or until the meat is almost tender. Add the potatoes and whole chillies and simmer until the potatoes are cooked.

Serves 4

Kofta Curry

SAUCE:
3 tablespoons oil
2.5 cm (1 inch) piece
  cinnamon stick*
10 cloves
1 onion, chopped
2 cloves garlic, finely
  chopped
5 cm (2 inch) piece
  ginger*, chopped
1 tablespoon ground
  cumin seeds*
2 tablespoons ground
  coriander seeds*
1 teaspoon chilli
  powder*
salt
1 × 397 g (14 oz)
  can tomatoes
KOFTA:
750 g (1½ lb)
  minced beef
2 green chillies*,
  finely chopped
3 tablespoons finely
  chopped coriander*
1 teaspoon garam
  masala*
1 egg, lightly beaten

Heat the oil in a large lidded frying pan. Add the cinnamon and cloves and fry for 30 seconds, then add the onion and fry until golden, stirring occasionally. Add the garlic, ginger, cumin, coriander, chilli powder and salt to taste. Stir well and fry over low heat for 2 minutes, adding 1-2 tablespoons water if the mixture begins to stick. Add the tomatoes with their juice and stir well. Cover and leave to simmer while preparing the Kofta. Mix the Kofta ingredients together, adding salt to taste. With dampened hands, shape the mixture into about 40 walnut-sized balls. Slip them carefully into the sauce in a single layer and simmer very gently for about 30 minutes, turning the meat balls over very carefully every 10 minutes.
Serves 4

Beef Buffad

3 tablespoons oil
2 onions, sliced
2 cloves garlic, finely
  chopped
3 green chillies*,
  chopped
3.5 cm (1½ inch)
  piece ginger*,
  chopped
750g (1½lb) braising
  steak, cubed
½ teaspoon chilli
  powder*
1 teaspoon turmeric*
1 teaspoon pepper
1 teaspoon ground
  cumin seeds*
1 tablespoon ground
  coriander seeds*
½ teaspoon ground
  cinnamon*
½ teaspoon ground
  cloves
300 ml (½ pint)
  coconut milk*
  (see note)
salt
150 ml (¼ pint)
  vinegar

Heat the oil in a large saucepan, add the onions and fry until they are just beginning to brown, then add the garlic, chillies and ginger. Fry for 1 minute, then add the beef and remaining spices. Stir well and cook for 5 minutes, stirring occasionally.

Add the coconut milk, which should just cover the meat; if it does not, add a little water. Add salt to taste. Bring to simmering point, cover and cook for about 1½ hours, until the meat is almost tender.

Add the vinegar and continue cooking for about 30 minutes, until the meat is tender and the gravy thick.

Serves 4

NOTE: 75 g (3 oz) creamed coconut*, melted in 250 ml (8 fl oz) warm water, can be used instead of coconut milk.

27

Nargis Kebab

KEBAB:
250 g (8 oz) ground
  beef or minced
  lamb
2 cloves garlic,
  crushed
2.5 cm (1 inch) piece
  ginger*, grated
½ teaspoon ground
  coriander seeds*
½ teaspoon ground
  cumin seeds*
½-1 teaspoon chilli
  powder*
¼ teaspoon ground
  cloves
1 tablespoon cornflour
salt
1 egg yolk
4 small hard-boiled
  eggs
oil for shallow frying
CURRY SAUCE:
4 tablespoons oil
5 cm (2 inch) piece
  cinnamon stick*
6 cloves
6 cardamom*
1 onion, finely
  chopped
2 cloves garlic,
  crushed
2.5 cm (1 inch) piece
  ginger*, grated
2 teaspoons ground
  coriander seeds*
1 teaspoon ground
  cumin seeds*
½-1 teaspoon chilli
  powder*
4 tablespoons natural
  yogurt
1 × 397 g (14 oz)
  can tomatoes
2 tablespoons
  chopped coriander*

Mix together the meat, garlic, spices, cornflour and salt to taste. Bind with the egg yolk and divide the mixture into 4 equal parts.

With well floured hands, flatten each portion into a round, place a hard-boiled egg in the centre and work the meat round to cover. Roll into a ball.

Heat the oil in a pan and shallow fry the kebabs until they are brown all over. Lift out and set aside while making the sauce.

Heat the oil in a saucepan, add the cinnamon, cloves and cardamom and fry for a few seconds. Add the onion, garlic and ginger and fry until golden brown. Add the coriander, cumin and chilli powder and fry for 1 minute. Add the yogurt, a spoonful at a time, stirring until it is absorbed before adding the next spoonful.

Break up the tomatoes with a fork, add them with their juice and simmer for 1 minute. Add the kebabs to the sauce, season with salt to taste and cook, uncovered, for 25 minutes until the sauce is thick. Stir in the chopped coriander to serve.

Serves 4

NOTE: The kebabs can also be served without the curry sauce, as part of a meal.

Kheema Do Pyaza

500 g (1 lb) onions
4 tablespoons oil
2.5 cm (1 inch) piece
    ginger*, chopped
1 clove garlic, finely
    chopped
2 green chillies*,
    finely chopped
1 teaspoon turmeric*
1 teaspoon ground
    coriander seeds*
1 teaspoon ground
    cumin seeds*
750 g (1½ lb)
    minced lamb
150 g (5.2 oz)
    natural yogurt
1 × 227 g (8 oz) can
    tomatoes
salt

Finely chop 350 g (12 oz) of the
onions; thinly slice the remainder.

Heat 2 tablespoons of the oil in a
pan, add the chopped onion and fry
until golden. Add the ginger, garlic,
chillies and spices and fry for
2 minutes. Add the minced lamb and
cook, stirring to break up, until well
browned.

Stir in the yogurt, spoon by spoon,
until it is absorbed, then add the
tomatoes with their juice, and salt to
taste. Bring to boil, stir well, cover
and simmer for 20 minutes or until
the meat is cooked.

Meanwhile fry the sliced onions in
the remaining oil until brown and crisp.

Transfer the meat mixture to a
warmed serving dish and sprinkle
with the fried onion.

Serves 4

Lamb Kebab

2 × 150 g (5.2 oz)
  cartons natural
  yogurt
1 tablespoon ground
  coriander seeds*
½ teaspoon chilli
  powder*
1 tablespoon oil
salt
750 g (1½ lb) boned
  leg of lamb, cubed
4 onions
2 red peppers, cored
  and seeded
4 tomatoes
2 tablespoons finely
  chopped coriander*

Put the yogurt, coriander seeds, chilli, oil, and salt to taste in a large bowl and stir to combine. Add the meat, mix well, cover and leave in the refrigerator overnight.

Cut the onions in quarters and separate the layers. Cut the peppers into squares and the tomatoes in half.

Thread the onion, lamb and red pepper alternately on 8 skewers, beginning and ending each kebab with a tomato half. Cook under a preheated hot grill for about 10 minutes, turning frequently and basting with any remaining marinade as necessary. Sprinkle with the chopped coriander to serve.

Serves 4

Lamb Curry with Coconut

grated flesh of ½
  fresh coconut*
4 dried red chillies*
1 teaspoon cumin seeds*
1 tablespoon
  coriander seeds*
1 tablespoon poppy
  seeds
1 teaspoon peppercorns
2.5 cm (½ inch) piece
  ginger*, chopped
2 cloves garlic
1 teaspoon turmeric*
2 tablespoons lemon
  juice
4 tablespoons oil
2 onions, chopped
4 curry leaves*
750 g (1½ lb) boned
  leg of lamb, cubed
1 × 227g (8 oz) can
  tomatoes
salt
2 tablespoons finely
  chopped coriander*

Heat the coconut, chillies, cumin, coriander and poppy seeds in a dry frying pan for about 1 minute. Place in an electric blender or food processor with the peppercorns, ginger, garlic, turmeric and lemon juice and blend to a paste.

Heat the oil in a pan, add the onions and fry until soft, then add the curry leaves and the prepared paste and fry for 5 minutes. Add the lamb and cook, stirring, for 5 minutes, then add the tomatoes with their juice and salt to taste. Bring to simmering point, cover and cook for about 1 hour, until tender.

Sprinkle with chopped coriander to serve.

Serves 4

NOTE: If fresh coconut is not available, blend the other spices and lemon juice as above and add 50 g (2 oz) creamed coconut* to the onions with the blended spices.

Roghan Ghosht

4 tablespoons oil
2 onions, finely
   chopped
750 g (1½ lb) boned
   leg of lamb, cubed
2 × 150 g (5.2 oz)
   cartons natural
   yogurt
2 cloves garlic
2.5 cm (1 inch) piece
   ginger*
2 green chillies*
1 tablespoon
   coriander seeds*
1 teaspoon cumin
   seeds*
1 teaspoon chopped
   mint leaves
1 teaspoon chopped
   coriander*
6 cardamom*
6 cloves
2.5 cm (1 inch) piece
   cinnamon stick*
salt
125 g (4 oz) flaked
   almonds

Heat 2 tablespoons of the oil in a pan, add one onion and fry until golden. Add the lamb and 175 g (6 oz) of the yogurt, stir well, cover and simmer for 20 minutes.

Place the garlic, ginger, chillies, coriander seeds, cumin, mint, coriander and 2 to 3 tablespoons yogurt in an electric blender or food processor and work to a paste.

Heat the remaining oil in a large saucepan, add the cardamom, cloves and cinnamon and fry for 1 minute, stirring. Add the second onion, prepared paste and fry for 5 minutes, stirring constantly.

Add the lamb and yogurt mixture, and salt to taste, stir well and bring to simmering point. Cover and cook for 30 minutes. Add the almonds and cook for a further 15 minutes, until the meat is tender.

Serves 4

Lamb Curry with Yogurt

4 tablespoons oil
3 onions, finely
    chopped
6 cardamom*
5 cm (2 inch) piece
    cinnamon stick*
1½ tablespoons
    ground coriander
    seeds*
2 teaspoons ground
    cumin seeds*
½ teaspoon turmeric*
½ teaspoon ground
    cloves
1-2 teaspoons chilli
    powder*
½ teaspoon grated
    nutmeg
1 tablespoon paprika
2 × 150 g (5.2 oz)
    cartons natural
    yogurt
750 g (1½ lb) boned
    leg of lamb, cubed
1 large tomato, skinned
    and chopped
salt

Heat the oil in a large saucepan, add the onions, cardamom and cinnamon and fry until onions turn golden. Stir in the coriander, cumin, turmeric, cloves, chilli powder and nutmeg. Fry until dry, then add 2 tablespoons water and cook, stirring, for 5 minutes, adding a little more water if necessary.

Add the paprika and slowly stir in the yogurt. Add the lamb, tomato, and salt to taste and mix well. Bring to simmering point, cover and cook for 1 hour or until the meat is tender.
Serves 4

Lamb Korma

5 tablespoons oil
6 cardamom*
6 cloves
6 peppercorns
2.5 cm (1 inch) piece
  cinnamon stick*
750 g (1½ lb) boned
  leg of lamb, cubed
6 shallots, chopped
2 cloves garlic, finely
  chopped
5 cm (2 inch) piece
  ginger*, chopped
2 tablespoons ground
  coriander seeds*
2 teaspoons ground
  cumin seeds*
1 teaspoon chilli
  powder*
salt
150 g (5.2 oz)
  natural yogurt
1 teaspoon garam
  masala*
2 tablespoons finely
  chopped coriander*
  (optional)

Heat 4 tablespoons of the oil in a pan, add the cardamom, cloves, peppercorns and cinnamon and fry for 1 minute.

Add a few pieces of lamb at a time and fry well to brown all over; transfer to a dish. Remove the whole spices and discard.

Add the remaining oil to the pan and fry the shallots, garlic and ginger for 5 minutes, then add the coriander, cumin, chilli powder, and salt to taste and cook for 5 minutes, stirring to avoid burning. Gradually stir in the yogurt until it is all absorbed.

Return the meat to the pan with any liquid collected in the dish and add sufficient water just to cover the meat. Bring to simmering point, cover and cook for about 1 hour or until the meat is tender.

Sprinkle on the garam masala and cook, stirring, for 1 minute. Top with chopped coriander if using, before serving.

Serves 4

Dry Lamb Curry

750 g (1½ lb) boned
    leg of lamb
3 tablespoons oil
250 g (8 oz) onions,
    finely chopped
6 cloves
6 cardamom
2.5 cm (1 inch) piece
    cinnamon stick*
2 green chillies*,
    finely chopped
2 teaspoons ground
    coriander seeds*
1 teaspoon ground
    cumin seeds*
2 × 150 g (5.2 oz)
    cartons natural
    yogurt
2 tablespoons finely
    chopped coriander*
3 curry leaves*
salt
1 teaspoon garam
    masala*

Cut the lamb into strips.

Heat the oil in a pan, add the onion and fry until soft. Add the cloves, cardamom and cinnamon and fry for 1 minute, then add the chillies and lamb. Fry for a further 10 minutes, turning the lamb to brown on all sides. Add the remaining ingredients, except the garam masala, seasoning with salt to taste. Stir well, bring to simmering point and cook, uncovered, for 40 minutes, until the meat is tender and the liquid evaporated. Stir in the garam masala and serve.

Serves 4

Masala Chops

1 teaspoon ground
  cumin seeds*
2 teaspoons ground
  coriander seeds*
1/4 teaspoon chilli
  powder*
1 clove garlic, crushed
salt
lemon juice to mix
4 pork chops

Mix the spices, garlic, and salt to taste into a paste with lemon juice. Slash the pork chops on both sides. Rub the paste into the meat and leave for 30 minutes. Cook under a preheated moderate grill for 5 or 6 minutes on each side.

Serves 4

Raan

2.25 kg (5 lb) leg of
  lamb, skin and fat
  removed
50 g (2 oz) fresh
  ginger*, chopped
6 cloves garlic
rind of 1 lemon
juice of 2 lemons
2 teaspoons cumin
  seeds*
6 cardamom*, peeled
1 teaspoon ground
  cloves
1 teaspoon turmeric*
1½ teaspoons chilli
  powder*
1 tablespoon salt
2 × 150 g (5.2 oz)
  cartons natural
  yogurt
150 g (5 oz) whole,
  unpeeled almonds
4 tablespoons brown
  sugar
1 teaspoon saffron
  threads*, soaked in
  3 tablespoons
  boiling water

Prick the lamb all over with a fork and make about 12 deep cuts.

Blend the ginger, garlic, lemon rind and juice, spices and salt in an electric blender or food processor. Spread over the lamb and leave to stand for 1 hour in a flameproof casserole.

Blend 4 tablespoons of the yogurt with the almonds and 2 tablespoons of the sugar. Stir in the remaining yogurt and pour over the lamb. Cover tightly and leave for 48 hours in the refrigerator.

Let the meat return to room temperature. Sprinkle over the remaining sugar and cook, uncovered, in a preheated hot oven, 220°C (425°F), Gas Mark 7, for 30 minutes. Cover, lower the temperature to 160°C (325°F), Gas Mark 3, and cook for 3 hours, basting occasionally. Sprinkle the saffron water over the meat and cook for a further 30 minutes or until very tender.

Remove the meat from the pan, wrap it in foil and keep warm. Skim off the fat from the casserole and boil the sauce until thick. Place the meat on a dish and pour over the sauce. Carve in thick slices to serve.

Serves 6

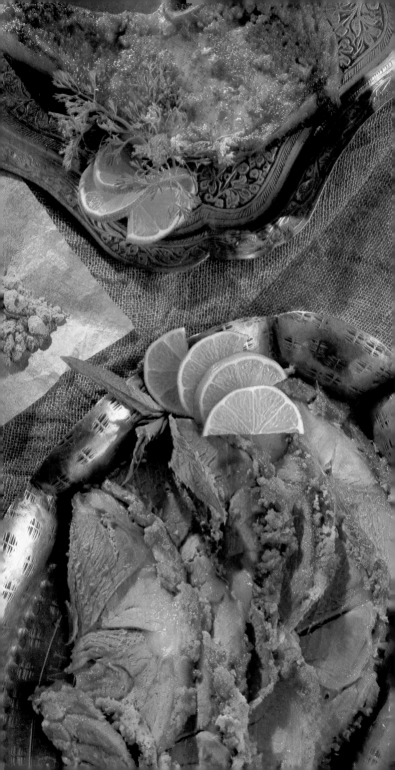

Pork Vindaloo

1-2 teaspoons chilli
  powder*
1 teaspoon turmeric*
2 teaspoons ground
  cumin seeds*
2 teaspoons ground
  mustard seed*
2 tablespoons ground
  coriander seeds*
3.5 cm (1½ inch)
  piece ginger*,
  finely chopped
salt
150 ml (¼ pint)
  vinegar
1 large onion, finely
  chopped
2 cloves garlic,
  crushed
750 g (1½ lb) pork
  fillet, cubed
4 tablespoons oil

Mix the spices, and salt to taste with
the vinegar. Put the onion, garlic and
pork in a bowl, pour over the vinegar
mixture, cover and leave in the
refrigerator overnight.

Heat the oil in a large saucepan,
add the pork mixture, bring to
simmering point, cover and cook for
about 45 minutes or until the pork is
tender.

Serves 4

Hurry Curry

500 g (1 lb) stewing
   beef, lamb or pork,
   cubed
500 g (1 lb) onions,
   finely chopped
2.5 cm (1 inch) piece
   cinnamon stick*
6 cloves
1 tablespoon ground
   coriander seeds*
1 teaspoon ground
   cumin seeds*
½ teaspoon turmeric*
1 teaspoon chilli
   powder*
2.5 cm (1 inch) piece
   ginger*, finely
   chopped
1 tablespoon tomato
   purée
3 tablespoons oil
salt
250 g (8 oz) small
   new potatoes
   (optional)

Put all the ingredients except the potatoes in a saucepan, seasoning with salt to taste. Stir well. The mixture should be moist; add an extra tablespoon of oil if necessary. Cover the pan tightly and leave overnight in the refrigerator.

Cook over a moderately high heat until the mixture starts to fry briskly. Stir well, then lower the heat and simmer for about 1½ hours or until the meat is tender.

Add the potatoes, if using, about 20 minutes before the end of the cooking time.

Serves 4

POULTRY DISHES

Kashmiri Chicken

125 g (4 oz) butter
3 large onions, finely
  sliced
10 peppercorns
10 cardamom*
5 cm (2 inch) piece
  cinnamon stick
5 cm (2 inch) piece
  ginger*, chopped
2 cloves garlic, finely
  chopped
1 teaspoon chilli
  powder*
2 teaspoons paprika
salt
1.5 kg (3 lb) chicken
  pieces, skinned
250 g (8 oz) natural
  yogurt

Melt the butter in a deep, lidded frying pan. Add the onions, peppercorns, cardamom and cinnamon and fry until the onions are golden. Add the ginger, garlic, chilli powder, paprika and salt to taste and fry for 2 minutes, stirring occasionally. Add the chicken pieces and fry until browned. Gradually add the yogurt, stirring constantly. Cover and cook gently for about 30 minutes.

Serves 6

Chicken Curry

2 cloves garlic,
  chopped
5 cm (2 inch) piece
  ginger*, chopped
1 teaspoon turmeric*
2 teaspoons cumin
  seeds*, ground
1 teaspoon chilli
  powder*
1 teaspoon pepper
3 tablespoons finely
  chopped coriander*
500 g (1 lb) natural
  yogurt
salt
1 kg (2 lb) chicken
  pieces, skinned
4 tablespoons oil
2 onions, chopped

Place the garlic, ginger, turmeric, cumin, chilli, pepper, coriander, yogurt and salt to taste in a large bowl. Mix well, add the chicken and leave for 4 hours, turning occasionally.

Heat the oil in a pan, add the onion and fry until golden. Add the chicken and the marinade. Bring to simmering point, cover and cook for about 30 minutes, until the chicken is tender.

Serves 4

Chicken and Dhal Curry

*250 g (8 oz) masoor
  dhal**
600 ml (1 pint) water
salt
3 tablespoons oil
2 onions, minced
*2 cloves garlic,
  minced*
*2.5 cm (1 inch) piece
  ginger*, minced*
*1 tablespoon ground
  coriander seeds**
*1 teaspoon ground
  cumin seeds**
1/2 teaspoon turmeric*
*1/2 teaspoon ground
  cloves*
*2 teaspoons chilli
  powder**
*750 g (1 1/2 lb)
  chicken thighs*

Wash the dhal, soak in clean water for
1 hour, then drain and boil in the
water with 1 teaspoon salt added, for
about 1 hour, until soft. Drain and set
aside.

Heat the oil in a saucepan, add the
onion, garlic and ginger and fry for
about 5 minutes. Add the spices and
salt to taste and fry gently for 10
minutes; if the mixture becomes too
dry, add 2 tablespoons water. Add
the chicken and fry until golden all
over. Add the cooked dhal, cover and
simmer for about 30 minutes, or until
the chicken is tender.

Serves 4

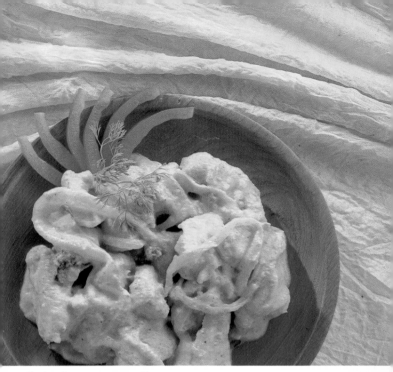

Chicken Molee

about 3 tablespoons oil
4 chicken breasts,
  skinned and boned,
  cut into 3 or 4 pieces
6 cardamom*
6 cloves
5 cm (2 inch) piece
  cinnamon stick*
1 large onion, finely
  sliced
2 cloves garlic
3.5 cm (1½ inch)
  piece ginger*,
  chopped
3 green chillies*,
  seeded
juice of 1 lemon
1 teaspoon turmeric*
50 g (2 oz) creamed
  coconut*
150 ml (¼ pint) hot
  water
salt

Heat the oil in a pan, add the chicken
and fry quickly all over. Remove
with a slotted spoon and set aside.

Add a little more oil to the pan if
necessary and fry the cardamom,
cloves and cinnamon for 1 minute.
Add the onion and fry until soft.

Place the garlic, ginger, chillies and
lemon juice in an electric blender or
food processor and work to a smooth
paste. Add to the pan with the
turmeric and cook for 5 minutes.

Melt the coconut in the hot water
and add to the pan with salt to taste.
Simmer for 2 minutes, then add the
chicken pieces and any juices.
Simmer for 15 to 20 minutes, until
tender.
Serves 4

Tandoori Chicken

½-1 teaspoon chilli
  powder*
1 teaspoon pepper
1 teaspoon salt
2 tablespoons lemon
  juice
1 × 1.5 kg (3 lb)
  oven-ready
  chicken, skinned
4 tablespoons natural
  yogurt
3 cloves garlic
5 cm (2 inch) piece
  ginger*
2 small dried red
  chillies*
1 tablespoon
  coriander seeds*
2 teaspoons cumin
  seeds*
50 g (2 oz) butter,
  melted

Mix the chilli powder, pepper, salt and lemon juice together. Slash the chicken all over and rub the mixture into the cuts. Set aside for 1 hour.

Place the yogurt, garlic, ginger, chillies, coriander and cumin in an electric blender or food processor and work to a paste. Spread it all over the chicken. Cover and leave in the refrigerator overnight. Return to room temperature before cooking.

Place on a rack in a roasting pan and pour over half the butter. Cook in a preheated moderately hot oven, 200°C (400°F), Gas Mark 6, for 1 hour or until tender. Baste occasionally and pour on the remaining butter halfway through cooking time.

Serves 4

NOTES: If preferred, the chicken can be spit-roasted for about 1 hour, using all the butter at the start.

The typical red colour of tandoori chicken is from a food colouring which is obtainable from Asian food shops. It has been omitted from this recipe, because many people are allergic to it.

Murgh Mussalam

2 onions
2 cloves garlic
5 cm (2 inch) piece
  ginger*
1 teaspoon poppy
  seeds
8 peppercorns
2 × 150 g (5.2 oz)
  cartons natural
  yogurt
1 teaspoon garam
  masala*
salt
1 × 1.5 kg (3 lb)
  oven-ready chicken
125 g (4 oz) long-
  grain rice, soaked
  in cold water for
  1 hour
3 tablespoons ghee*
½ teaspoon chilli
  powder*
50 g (2 oz) sultanas
50 g (2 oz) slivered
  almonds
350 ml (12 fl oz)
  water

Place the onions, garlic, ginger, poppy seeds, peppercorns and half the yogurt in an electric blender or food processor and work to a paste. Stir in the garam masala, add salt to taste.

Prick the chicken all over with a fork and rub in the blended mixture. Leave for 1 hour. Drain the rice.

Heat 1 tablespoon of the ghee in a pan, add the rice and fry for 3 minutes, stirring constantly. Add the chilli powder, sultanas, almonds and salt to taste and stir well. Pour in 175 ml (6 fl oz) of the water, cover and simmer for about 10 minutes, until the rice is almost tender; cool.

When the rice is cold, use it to stuff the chicken; sew up both ends. Heat the remaining ghee or oil in a pan and add the chicken, on its side. Pour in any marinade and the remaining water. Bring to simmering point, cover and cook for 1 hour, turning over halfway through cooking time.

Add the remaining yogurt, a spoonful at a time, stirring until it is all absorbed. Add more salt if necessary. Cook for a further 15 minutes, until the chicken is tender.
Serves 4

FISH DISHES

Fish Molee

750 g (1½ lb) cod
    fillet, skinned
2 tablespoons flour
4 tablespoons oil
2 onions, sliced
2 cloves garlic, crushed
1 teaspoon turmeric*
4 green chillies*,
    finely chopped
2 tablespoons lemon
    juice
175 ml (6 fl oz) thick
    coconut milk*
salt

Cut the fish into 4 pieces and coat with the flour. Heat the oil in a frying pan, add the fish and fry quickly on both sides. Remove with a slotted spoon and set aside.

Add the onion and garlic to the pan and fry until soft and golden. Add the turmeric, chillies, lemon juice, coconut milk, and salt to taste and simmer, uncovered, for 10 minutes or until thickened.

Add the fish and any juices, spoon over the sauce and cook gently for 2 to 3 minutes, until tender.

Serves 4

Baked Spiced Fish

4 tablespoons oil
125 g (4 oz) grated
   coconut*
5 cm (2 inch) piece
   ginger*, chopped
1 large onion,
   chopped
4 cloves garlic, finely
   chopped
2 green chillies*,
   seeded and chopped
1 teaspoon chilli
   powder*
2 tablespoons finely
   chopped coriander*
4 tablespoons lemon
   juice
salt
1 kg (2 lb) cod steaks

Heat the oil in a pan, add the coconut, ginger, onion, garlic, chillies and chilli powder and fry gently until the onion is translucent. Add the coriander, lemon juice and salt to taste and simmer for 15 minutes or until the coconut is soft.

Oil the bottom of a baking dish just large enough to hold the fish. Arrange the fish steaks side by side and pour over the spice mixture.

Bake in a preheated moderate oven, 160°C (325°F), Gas Mark 3, for 25 minutes or until tender.
Serves 4

Amotik

50 g (2 oz)
   tamarind*, soaked
   in 6 tablespoons
   hot water for
   30 minutes
4 tablespoons oil
750 g (1½ lb)
   monkfish or other
   firm white fish,
   cubed
flour for dusting
1 onion, chopped
4 green chillies*,
   finely chopped
2 cloves garlic,
   crushed
1 teaspoon ground
   cumin seeds*
½-1 teaspoon chilli
   powder*
salt
1 tablespoon vinegar

Strain the tamarind, squeezing out as much water as possible. Discard the tamarind and reserve the water.

Heat the oil in a large pan. Lightly dust the fish with flour, add to the pan and fry quickly on both sides. Remove from the pan with a slotted spoon and set aside.

Add the onion to the pan and fry until soft and golden. Add the tamarind water, chillies, garlic, cumin, chilli powder, and salt to taste and cook for 10 minutes. Add the fish and any juices and the vinegar. Simmer, uncovered, for about 5 minutes; be careful not to overcook.

Serves 4

Grilled Spiced Fish

2 large or 4 small
    plaice, cleaned
150 g (5.2 oz)
    natural yogurt
2 cloves garlic,
    crushed
1 teaspoon ground
    coriander seeds*
½ teaspoon chilli
    powder*
1 teaspoon garam
    masala*
1 tablespoon vinegar
    or lemon juice
1 tablespoon oil
salt
TO GARNISH:
2 tablespoons finely
    chopped parsley
1 lemon, quartered

Slash the fish on both sides and place
in separate shallow dishes. Mix the
remaining ingredients together,
adding salt to taste, and divide
between the fish. Spoon it all over
one side and leave for 1 hour, then
turn and spoon over the juice that has
collected in the dish. Leave for
another hour.

Cook under a preheated moderate
grill for 3 to 4 minutes. Turn and
baste with any juices collected in the
grill pan, then cook for a further 3 or
4 minutes.

Serve sprinkled with the parsley
and accompanied by lemon quarters.
Serves 4

Fish Fritters

6 tablespoons oil
2 onions, chopped
1 tablespoon ground
    coriander seeds*
3 green chillies*,
    seeded and chopped
1 teaspoon salt
1 teaspoon pepper
750 g (1½ lb) cod
    fillets, skinned and
    cut into small
    pieces
2 tablespoons finely
    chopped coriander*
BATTER:
125 g (4 oz) gram
    flour*
½ teaspoon chilli
    powder*
½ teaspoon salt
1 egg, beaten
7 tablespoons water

Heat 3 tablespoons of the oil in a pan, add the onion and fry until just soft. Stir in the coriander, chillies, salt and pepper, then add the fish. Fry for 2 minutes, then cover and cook on very low heat for 2 minutes. Break up the mixture with a fork and add the chopped coriander. Remove from the heat and set aside while making the batter.

Sift the flour, chilli powder and salt into a bowl. Add the egg and water and beat well to make a smooth batter. Leave to stand for 30 minutes, then stir in the fish mixture.

Heat the remaining oil in a frying pan and drop in small spoonfuls of the batter mixture. Fry on both sides until golden. Drain thoroughly and keep warm while frying the remainder.

Serves 4

Pickled Haddock Steaks

4 tablespoons oil
4 haddock steaks, each
    weighing about
    250 g (8 oz),
    cleaned
2 onions, chopped
2 cloves garlic
2.5 cm (1 inch) piece
    ginger*
1 tablespoon
    coriander seeds*
4 green chillies*,
    seeded
5 tablespoons vinegar
½ teaspoon turmeric*
4 curry leaves*
salt

Heat the oil in a large frying pan, add the fish and fry on both sides until browned. Remove with a slotted spoon and set aside. Add the onions to the pan and fry until soft.

Place the garlic, ginger, coriander seeds, chillies and 1 tablespoon of the vinegar in an electric blender or food processor and work to a paste. Add to the pan with the turmeric, curry leaves, and salt to taste and fry for 3 to 4 minutes.

Add the remaining vinegar, bring to simmering point, stir well and add the fish. Cook, uncovered, for 3 to 4 minutes, until tender.

Place the fish in a dish, pour over all the juices and leave to cool. Cover and keep in the refrigerator for at least 12 hours. Serve cold.
Serves 4

VEGETABLE DISHES

Spicy Turnips

about 3 tablespoons
    ghee*
1 kg (2 lb) turnips,
    quartered
2 cloves garlic
2 green chillies*
2.5 cm (1 inch) piece
    ginger*
1 teaspoon cumin
    seeds*
2 teaspoons coriander
    seeds*
2 tablespoons natural
    yogurt
1 teaspoon salt
150ml (¼pint) water
1 teaspoon sugar
1 teaspoon garam
    masala*

Heat the ghee in a pan, add the turnips and fry lightly; set aside.

Place the garlic, chillies, ginger, cumin, coriander and yogurt in an electric blender or food processor and work to a paste. Add to the pan, adding more ghee if necessary, and fry for 2 minutes.

Return the turnips to the pan, add the salt and stir well. Add the water and simmer, covered, for about 10 minutes, until almost tender. Uncover the pan, add the sugar and garam masala and cook briskly, stirring, until most of the liquid has evaporated.

Serves 4 to 6

Tomato and Coriander

3 tablespoons oil or
  ghee*
2 onions, chopped
1 kg (2 lb) tomatoes,
  sliced
2.5 cm (1 inch) piece
  ginger*, chopped
1 teaspoon ground
  cumin seeds*
1 teaspoon ground
  coriander seeds*
½ teaspoon chilli
  powder*
1 teaspoon salt
3 green chillies*
1 teaspoon sugar
50 g (2 oz) coriander*,
  finely chopped

Heat the oil or ghee in a pan, add the
onions and fry until soft. Add the
tomatoes, ginger, cumin, coriander,
chilli powder, and salt and simmer,
uncovered, until the mixture begins
to thicken. Add the chillies and sugar
and continue cooking for 5 to
10 minutes, until fairly thick. Stir in
the coriander and serve.
Serves 4

Phul Gobi with Peppers

3 tablespoons oil
1 onion, sliced
½ teaspoon turmeric*
1 cauliflower, broken
　　into florets
salt
2 green chillies*,
　　seeded
1 green, 1 yellow and
　　1 red pepper,
　　cored, seeded and
　　cut into strips

Heat the oil in a pan, add the onion and fry until soft. Add the turmeric and cook for 1 minute. Add the cauliflower and salt to taste, stir well, cover and cook gently for about 10 minutes, until the cauliflower is almost cooked.

Add the chillies and peppers, stir and cook for a further 5 minutes or until tender.

Serves 4

Aloo Mattar

5 tablespoons oil
1 onion, chopped
2.5 cm (1 inch) piece
　　ginger*, chopped
1 green chilli*, finely
　　chopped
2 cloves garlic, crushed
1 teaspoon turmeric*
750 g (1½ lb)
　　potatoes, cut into
　　small cubes
salt
6-8 mint leaves
250 g (8 oz) shelled
　　or frozen peas

Heat the oil in a pan, add the onion and fry until soft and translucent. Add the ginger, chilli, garlic and turmeric, stir well and cook for 5 minutes. Add the potatoes and salt to taste, stir well, cover and cook for 5 minutes.

Add the mint and fresh peas, stir well and cook for 20 minutes, until tender. If using frozen peas, add them after the potatoes have cooked for 15 minutes and cook for 3 minutes only.

Serves 4 to 6

Gobi ki Foogath

3 tablespoons oil
1 onion, finely sliced
2 cloves garlic, crushed
3 green chillies*,
　　seeded and finely
　　chopped
2.5 cm (1 inch) piece
　　ginger*, finely
　　chopped
500 g (1 lb) white
　　cabbage, finely
　　sliced
salt

Heat the oil in a large pan, add the onion and fry until just soft. Add the garlic, chillies and ginger and cook for 1 minute. Add the cabbage, with the water clinging to the leaves after washing, and salt to taste. Stir very well, cover and cook, stirring occasionally, for about 15 minutes; the cabbage should still be slightly crunchy. If liquid gathers, uncover the pan for the last 5 minutes to allow it to evaporate.

Serves 4

Masoor Dhal

4 tablespoons oil
6 cloves
6 cardamom*
2.5 cm (1 inch) piece
   cinnamon stick*
1 onion, chopped
2.5 cm (1 inch) piece
   ginger*, chopped
1 green chilli*, finely
   chopped
1 clove garlic,
   chopped
½ teaspoon garam
   masala*
250 g (8 oz) masoor
   dhal*
salt
juice of 1 lemon

Heat the oil in a pan, add the cloves, cardamom and cinnamon and fry until they start to swell. Add the onion and fry until translucent. Add ginger, chilli, garlic and garam masala and cook for about 5 minutes.

Add the lentils, stir thoroughly and fry for 1 minute. Add salt to taste and enough water to come about 3 cm (1¼ inches) above the level of the lentils. Bring to the boil, cover and simmer for about 20 minutes, until really thick and tender.

Sprinkle with the lemon juice, stir and serve immediately.
Serves 4

Panir Mattar

125 g (4 oz) panir*
2-3 tablespoons oil
2 tablespoons finely
   chopped onion
90 ml (3 fl oz) water
salt
250 g (8 oz) shelled
   peas
1/2 teaspoon sugar
1 tablespoon grated
   ginger*
2 green chillies*,
   finely chopped
1/2 teaspoon garam
   masala*
1 tablespoon finely
   chopped coriander*

Cut the panir into 1 cm (1/2 inch) cubes. Heat the oil in a heavy-based pan, add the panir and fry until golden, turning gently and taking care not to burn. Remove from the pan and set aside. Add the onions to the pan and fry until coloured; remove and set aside.

Add the water, and salt to taste, to the pan and bring to the boil. Add the peas and sugar, cover and simmer until the peas are almost tender. If necessary, uncover and cook for 1 minute to evaporate any liquid.

Add the onions, ginger and chillies and stir well. Cook for 2 minutes, then very gently stir in the panir. Heat through for 2 minutes, then stir in the garam masala and coriander. Serve immediately.
Serves 4

Sprouting Mung Dhal

250 g (8 oz) whole
    mung beans, rinsed
3-4 tablespoons oil
1 onion, thinly sliced
2 green chillies*,
    seeded and chopped
2.5 cm (1 inch) piece
    ginger*, cut into
    fine matchsticks
1 teaspoon fennel
    seeds*
salt
300 ml (½ pint)
    water

A day in advance, put the beans in a bowl and barely cover them with warm water. Cover the bowl with cling wrap and leave in a warm dark place. Do not let the beans dry out; add a little extra water if necessary. The beans will have sprouted by the next day. Rinse and drain them.

Heat the oil in a saucepan. Add the onion and fry, stirring, for 3 minutes. Stir in the chillies, ginger, and fennel seeds and cook, stirring, until the onions have softened a little.

Add the beans, salt to taste and the water. Bring to simmering point, cover and cook gently, stirring occasionally, for 25 to 30 minutes or until the beans are soft and there is no liquid left.
Serves 4

Courgette, Peas and Coriander

4 tablespoons oil
2 onions, sliced
2 cloves garlic, finely
    chopped
2 green chillies*,
    chopped
2.5 cm (1 inch) piece
    ginger*, chopped
4 tablespoons finely
    chopped coriander*
salt
500 g (1 lb)
    courgettes, cut into
    5 mm (¼ inch)
    slices
250 g (8 oz) shelled
    peas

Heat the oil in a pan, add the onion and fry until soft. Add the garlic, chillies, ginger, coriander and salt to taste and cook for 5 minutes, stirring occasionally. Add the courgettes and peas, stir well, cover and cook for 30 minutes, or until the peas are tender. If necessary, boil quickly to evaporate any liquid before serving.
Serves 4

Aloo Sag

6 tablespoons oil
1 onion, chopped
2.5 cm (1 inch) piece
    ginger*, chopped
2 green chillies*,
    finely chopped
1 teaspoon turmeric*
2 cloves garlic, finely
    chopped
500 g (1 lb) potatoes,
    cut into small pieces
salt
2 × 227 g (8 oz)
    packets frozen
    spinach leaf,
    thawed

Heat the oil in a lidded frying pan,
add the onion and cook until soft.
Add the spices and garlic and cook for
5 minutes. Add the potatoes, and salt
to taste, stir well, cover and cook for
10 minutes.

Squeeze out any liquid from the
spinach and chop. Add to the
potatoes and cook for about
5 minutes, until both vegetables are
tender.
Serves 4

Tamatar Aloo

2 tablespoons oil
1/2 teaspoon mustard
    seeds*
250 g (8 oz)
    potatoes, cut into
    small cubes
1 teaspoon turmeric*
1 teaspoon chilli
    powder*
2 teaspoons paprika
juice of 1 lemon
1 teaspoon sugar
salt
250 g (8 oz) tomatoes,
    quartered
2 tablespoons finely
    chopped coriander*
    to garnish

Heat the oil in a pan, add the mustard
seeds and fry until they pop – just a
few seconds. Add the potatoes and
fry for about 5 minutes. Add the
spices, lemon juice, sugar and salt
to taste, stir well and cook for
5 minutes.

Add the tomatoes, stir well, then
simmer for 5 to 10 minutes until the
potatoes are tender.

Sprinkle with coriander to serve.
Serves 4

Dhai Aloo

4 tablespoons oil
1 onion, chopped
2.5 cm (1 inch) piece
  ginger*, finely
  chopped
1 tablespoon ground
  coriander seeds*
2 green chillies*,
  finely chopped
750 g (1½ lb) small
  new potatoes
1 × 227 g (8 oz) can
  tomatoes
100 g (3½ oz) raisins
salt
2 × 150 g (5.2 oz)
  cartons natural
  yogurt
2 tablespoons chopped
  coriander* to
  garnish

Heat the oil in a large pan, add the onion and ginger and fry until soft. Stir in the coriander seeds and chillies and fry for 2 minutes. Add the potatoes, stir well, cover and cook very gently for 5 minutes, stirring occasionally so they colour evenly.

Add the tomatoes with their juice, raisins and salt to taste and stir well. Increase the heat a little and cook, uncovered. As the liquid evaporates, add half the yogurt, a tablespoon at a time. When the potatoes have cooked for 20 minutes and are just about ready, add the remaining yogurt, a tablespoon at a time, lower the heat and cook for 2 minutes. Sprinkle with coriander to serve.

Serves 4 to 6

69

Potato with Mustard Seed

4 tablespoons oil
1 teaspoon mustard
   seeds*
1 teaspoon turmeric*
1-2 green chillies*,
   chopped
500 g (1 lb) potatoes,
   boiled and diced
juice of 1 lemon
salt

Heat the oil in a frying pan and add the mustard seeds. When they begin to pop, stir in the turmeric and chillies and cook for a few seconds. Add the potatoes and stir well to mix. Pour in the lemon juice and add salt to taste. Stir well and heat through.
Serves 4

Bharta

500 g (1 lb)
   aubergines
2 tablespoons oil
1 large onion, finely
   chopped
1 clove garlic, crushed
1 green chilli*, seeded
   and chopped
1 tablespoon ground
   coriander seeds*
1 tablespoon finely
   chopped coriander*
salt
1 tablespoon lemon
   juice

Cook the aubergines in a preheated moderate oven, 180°C (350°F), Gas Mark 4, for 30 minutes or until soft. Cool slightly, then slit open, scoop out all the flesh and beat it with a fork.

   Heat the oil in a pan, add the onion, garlic and chilli and fry until the onion is soft but not coloured. Add the ground and fresh coriander and salt to taste. Add the aubergine pulp, stir well and fry, uncovered, for 2 minutes, then cover and simmer very gently for 5 minutes. Sprinkle with lemon juice and serve.
Serves 4

Dhai Bhindi

250 g (8 oz) okra
2 tablespoons oil
2.5 cm (1 inch) piece
   ginger*, chopped
1 teaspoon turmeric*
salt
2-3 tablespoons water
2 × 150 g (5.2 oz)
   cartons natural
   yogurt
1/2 teaspoon chilli
   powder*
2 tablespoons grated
   coconut*
1 tablespoon finely
   chopped coriander*

Cut the tops off the okra and halve them lengthways. Heat the oil in a pan, add the okra and fry for 5 minutes. Add the ginger, turmeric, and salt to taste, stir well, add the water, cover and cook for 10 minutes, until the okra is tender.

   Mix the remaining ingredients together; add to the pan, stir well and serve.
Serves 4

Kabli Channa

250 g (8 oz) whole
   Bengal gram*
750 ml (1¼ pints)
   water
1 teaspoon salt
2 tablespoons ghee*
   or oil
1 onion, chopped
2.5 cm (1 inch) piece
   cinnamon stick*
4 cloves
2 cloves garlic,
   crushed
2.5 cm (1 inch) piece
   ginger*, chopped
2 green chillies*,
   finely chopped
2 teaspoons ground
   coriander seeds
150 g (5 oz)
   tomatoes, chopped
1 teaspoon garam
   masala*
1 tablespoon finely
   chopped coriander*

Wash the gram and soak in the water
overnight. Add the salt and simmer
until tender. Drain, reserving the
water, and set aside.

Heat the ghee or oil in a pan, add
the onion and fry until golden. Add
the cinnamon and cloves and fry for a
few seconds, then add the garlic,
ginger, chillies and ground coriander
and fry for 5 minutes. Add the
tomatoes and fry until most of the
liquid has evaporated.

Add the gram and cook gently for
5 minutes, then add the reserved
water and simmer for 20 to 25
minutes. Add the garam masala and
stir well. Sprinkle with the chopped
coriander and serve immediately.
Serves 4

Vegetable Curry

3 tablespoons oil
1 teaspoon fennel
　seeds*
2 onions, sliced
1 teaspoon chilli
　powder*
1 tablespoon ground
　coriander seeds*
2.5 cm (1 inch) piece
　ginger*, chopped
salt
2 aubergines, sliced
175 g (6 oz) shelled
　peas
125 g (4 oz)
　potatoes, cubed
1 × 227 g (8 oz) can
　tomatoes
4 green chillies*

Heat the oil in a large pan, add the
fennel seeds and fry for a few
seconds, then add the onions and fry
until soft and golden. Add the chilli
powder, coriander, ginger and salt to
taste and fry for 2 minutes. Add the
aubergines, peas and potatoes and
cook for 5 minutes, stirring
occasionally.
　Add the tomatoes with their juice
and the chillies, cover and simmer
for 30 minutes, or until the peas are
tender and the sauce is thick.
Serves 4

RICE DISHES

Tomato Rice

250 g (8 oz) long-
   grain rice
3 tablespoons oil
1 onion, sliced
1 clove garlic, crushed
2.5 cm (1 inch) piece
   ginger*, chopped
1 × 539 g (1 lb 3 oz)
   can tomatoes
salt
2 tablespoons finely
   chopped coriander*

Wash the rice under running cold water, then soak in fresh cold water for 30 minutes; drain thoroughly.

Heat the oil in a large pan, add the onion and fry until golden. Add the garlic and ginger and fry for 2 minutes. Add the rice, stir well and fry for 2 minutes.

Break up the tomatoes in their juice and add to the rice with salt to taste. Bring to the boil, then cover and simmer for 15 to 20 minutes, until tender.

Transfer to a warmed serving dish and sprinkle with the coriander.
Serves 4

Kitcheri

175 g (6 oz) long-
    grain rice
175 g (6 oz) masoor
    dhal*
50 g (2 oz) butter
1 onion
1 clove garlic,
    chopped
5 cm (2 inch) piece
    cinnamon stick*
5 cardamom*
5 cloves
10 peppercorns
450 ml (¾ pint)
    boiling water
salt

Wash the combined rice and dhal
under running cold water, then leave
to soak in fresh cold water for
30 minutes.

Melt the butter in a large pan. Add
the onion to the pan with the garlic,
cinnamon, cardamom, cloves and
peppercorns. Fry gently until the
onion is soft.

Add the drained rice and dhal to
the pan and fry gently, stirring, for
2 minutes. Add the water, and salt to
taste and boil for 2 minutes. Cover
tightly and simmer for about 20
minutes, until the water is absorbed.

Transfer the rice mixture to a
warmed serving dish to serve.

Serves 4

NOTE: Kitcheri looks most attractive
garnished with crisply fried onion
rings.

Chicken Pilau

350 g (12 oz)
  Basmati rice
1 × 1.5 kg (3½ lb)
  oven-ready chicken
5 tablespoons ghee*
  or butter
5 cm (2 inch) piece
  cinnamon stick*
8 cloves
6 cardamom*
2 cloves garlic,
  crushed
½-1 teaspoon chilli
  powder*
1 tablespoon fennel
  seeds*
5 tablespoons natural
  yogurt
1 teaspoon powdered
  saffron*
1½ teaspoons salt
about 600 ml (1 pint)
  chicken stock
TO GARNISH:
4 tablespoons ghee*
  or butter
2 large onions, sliced

Wash the rice under cold water, then soak in fresh cold water for 30 minutes; drain thoroughly. Skin the chicken and cut into pieces.

Melt the ghee or butter in a large flameproof casserole. Add the cinnamon, cloves and cardamom and fry for 30 seconds. Stir in the garlic, chilli and fennel and fry for 30 seconds.

Add the chicken and fry, turning, for 5 minutes. Add the yogurt a spoonful at a time, stirring until absorbed before adding the next spoonful. Cover and simmer for 25 minutes or until tender.

Add the rice, saffron and salt. Fry, stirring, until the rice is well mixed and glistening. Add enough stock to cover the rice by 5 mm (¼ inch) and bring to the boil. Reduce the heat to very low, cover tightly and cook for 20 minutes or until the rice is cooked and the liquid absorbed.

Melt the ghee or butter in a small pan, add the onion and fry until golden. Transfer the pilau to a warmed dish, and garnish with the fried onion.
Serves 6

Boiled Rice

350 g (12 oz) long-
grain rice
450 ml (¾ pint)
water
salt

Wash the rice very thoroughly under running cold water, then soak in clean cold water for 30 minutes; drain.

Place in a large pan with the water and salt to taste and bring to the boil. Cover, turn down the heat to very low and cook for 20 to 25 minutes, until the rice is tender and the liquid absorbed.
Serves 4 to 6
Illustrated on pages 38 and 39

Prawn Pilau

350 g (12 oz)
Basmati rice
6 tablespoons ghee*
or butter
1 tablespoon
coriander seeds*,
crushed
½ teaspoon turmeric*
1 small pineapple,
cubed, or 1 × 227 g
(8 oz) can
pineapple cubes,
drained
227 g (8 oz) frozen
prawns, thawed
1 teaspoon salt
about 600 ml (1 pint)
fish or chicken
stock
TO GARNISH:
2 tablespoons ghee*
or butter
2 tablespoons
sultanas
2 tablespoons cashew
nuts
2 hard-boiled eggs,
quartered
2 tablespoons
chopped coriander*

Wash the rice under cold running water, then soak in fresh cold water for 30 minutes; drain thoroughly.

Melt the ghee or butter in a large saucepan, add the coriander seeds and fry for 30 seconds. Add the turmeric and stir for a few seconds, then add the pineapple and fry, stirring, for 30 seconds. Add the prawns, rice and salt. (If using a stock cube, omit the salt.) Fry, stirring, for 1 minute, then pour in enough stock to cover the rice by 5 mm (¼ inch). Bring to the boil, cover tightly and cook very gently for 25 minutes or until the rice is cooked and the liquid absorbed.

Meanwhile, prepare the garnish. Heat the ghee or butter in a small pan, add the sultanas and cashews and fry for 1 to 2 minutes, until the sultanas are plump and the nuts lightly coloured.

Transfer the rice to a warmed serving dish and gently fork in the sultanas and nuts. Arrange the egg around the edge and sprinkle the coriander on top.
Serves 6

Biryani

8 tablespoons ghee*
    or oil
10 cm (4 inch) piece
    cinnamon stick*
8 whole cardamom*
12 cloves
4 cloves garlic,
    crushed
3.5 cm (1½ inch)
    piece ginger*,
    chopped
1 teaspoon fennel
    seeds*
½ teaspoon chilli
    powder*
1 kg (2 lb) boned leg
    of lamb, cubed
2 × 150 g (5.2 oz)
    cartons natural
    yogurt
150 ml (¼ pint)
    water
2 teaspoons salt
500 g (1 lb) Basmati
    rice, washed and
    soaked for 30
    minutes
½ teaspoon saffron
    threads*, soaked in
    3 tablespoons
    boiling water
TO GARNISH:
2 tablespoons ghee*
    or oil
1 large onion, sliced
4 tablespoons flaked
    almonds
4 tablespoons
    sultanas

Heat 6 tablespoons of the ghee or oil in a large saucepan. Add the cinnamon, cardamom and cloves and fry for a few seconds, stirring. When the spices let out a strong aroma, stir in the garlic, ginger, fennel and chilli powder. Fry for 5 minutes, stirring constantly.

Add the lamb and fry well on all sides. Stir in the yogurt a tablespoon at a time, allowing each spoonful to be absorbed before adding the next. Add the water and half the salt, cover and simmer for 40 minutes or until the lamb is tender.

Meanwhile, fill another large pan two thirds full with water and bring to the boil. Drain the rice and add to the pan with the remaining salt. Boil for 3 minutes, then drain.

Put the remaining ghee or oil in a large casserole, cover the base with rice and sprinkle with the saffron water, then cover with a layer of lamb. Repeat the layers, finishing with rice. Pour in any liquid from the lamb, cover closely with a foil-lined lid and cook in a preheated moderately hot oven, 190°C (375°F), Gas Mark 5, for 25 to 30 minutes or until the rice is tender.

Meanwhile, prepare the garnish. Heat the ghee or oil in a small frying pan, add the onion and fry until golden. Remove from the pan and set aside. Add the almonds and sultanas to the pan and fry until the almonds are lightly coloured and the sultanas plump.

Transfer the biryani to a warmed serving dish and sprinkle with the onion, almonds and sultanas to serve.
Serves 4 to 6

Pilau Rice

3 tablespoons oil
5 cm (2 inch) piece
    cinnamon stick*
4 cardamom*
4 cloves
1 onion, sliced
250 g (8 oz) long-
    grain rice, washed
    and soaked for
    30 minutes
600 ml (1 pint) beef
    stock or water
salt

Heat the oil in a casserole, add the cinnamon, cardamom and cloves and fry for a few seconds. Add the onion and fry until golden. Drain the rice thoroughly, add to the pan and fry, stirring occasionally, for 5 minutes. Add the stock or water, and salt to taste. Bring to the boil, then simmer, uncovered, for 10 minutes, until the rice is tender and the liquid absorbed.

Serves 4

Illustrated on page 26

VARIATION:

Vegetable Pilau: Add 125 g (4 oz) each shelled peas, thinly sliced carrots and cauliflower florets to the pan after frying the onion. Fry for 5 minutes, then add the rice and proceed as above.

79

BREADS

Paratha

250 g (8 oz)
   wholemeal flour
1 teaspoon salt
200 ml (⅓ pint)
   water
   (approximately)
50-75 g (2-3 oz)
   melted ghee* or
   butter

Make the dough as for Chapati
(opposite) and divide into 6 pieces.
Roll out each piece on a floured
surface into a thin circle. Brush with
melted ghee or butter and fold in half;
brush again and fold in half again.
Roll out again to a circle about 3 mm
(⅛ inch) thick.

   Lightly grease a griddle or heavy-
based frying pan with a little ghee or
butter and place over a moderate
heat. Add a paratha and cook for
1 minute. Lightly brush the top with
a little ghee or butter and turn over.
Brush all round the edge with ghee or
butter and cook until golden.
Remove from the pan and keep warm
while cooking the rest. Serve hot.
Makes 6

Chapati

250 g (8 oz)
  wholemeal flour
1 teaspoon salt
200 ml (⅓ pint)
  water
  (approximately)

Place the flour and salt in a bowl. Make a well in the centre, gradually stir in the water and work to a soft supple dough. Knead for 10 minutes, then cover and leave in a cool place for 30 minutes. Knead again very thoroughly, then divide into 12 pieces. Roll out each piece on a floured surface into a thin round pancake.

Lightly grease a griddle or heavy-based frying pan with a little ghee* or oil and place over a moderate heat. Add a chapati and cook until blisters appear. Press down with a fish slice, then turn and cook the other side until lightly coloured. Remove from the pan and keep warm while cooking the rest.

Brush a little butter on one side and serve warm.

Makes 12

Puri

250 g (8 oz)
wholemeal flour,
or half wholemeal
and half plain
white
¼ teaspoon salt
150 ml (¼ pint)
warm water
(approximately)
2 teaspoons melted
ghee*
oil for deep-frying

Place the wholemeal flour and salt in a bowl; sift in the plain flour if using. Make a well in the centre, add the water gradually and work to a dough. Knead in the ghee, then knead for 10 minutes, until smooth and elastic. Cover and set aside for 30 minutes.

Divide the dough into 16 pieces. With lightly oiled hands, pat each piece into a ball. Lightly oil the pastry board and rolling pin and roll out each ball into a thin circular pancake.

Deep-fry the puris very quickly, turning them over once, until deep golden in colour. Drain well and serve immediately.
Makes 16

Naan

15 g (1/2 oz) fresh
    yeast
1/4 teaspoon sugar
2 tablespoons warm
    water
500 g (1 lb) self-
    raising flour
1 teaspoon salt
150 ml (1/4 pint)
    tepid milk
150 ml (1/4 pint)
    natural yogurt (at
    room temperature)
2 tablespoons melted
    butter or cooking
    oil
TO GARNISH:
2-3 tablespoons
    melted butter
1 tablespoon poppy
    or sesame seeds

Put the yeast in a small bowl with the sugar and water. Mix well until the yeast has dissolved, then leave in a warm place for 15 minutes or until the mixture is frothy.

Sift the flour and salt into a large bowl. Make a well in the centre and pour in the yeast, milk, yogurt and butter or oil. Mix well to a smooth dough and turn onto a floured surface. Knead well for about 10 minutes, until smooth and elastic. Place in the bowl, cover with clingfilm and leave to rise in a warm place for 1 to 1½ hours, or until doubled in size.

Turn onto a floured surface, knead for a few minutes, then divide into 6 pieces. Pat or roll each piece into a round.

Place on a warmed baking sheet and bake in a preheated very hot oven, 240°C (475°F), Gas Mark 9, for 10 minutes. Brush with butter and sprinkle with the poppy or sesame seeds. Serve warm.
Makes 6

ACCOMPANIMENTS

Carrot Salad

125 g (4 oz) carrots,
  grated
25 g (1 oz) grated
  onion
½ tablespoon grated
  ginger*
1 tablespoon finely
  chopped mint
½ teaspoon salt
½ teaspoon sugar
1 tablespoon lemon
  juice

Mix all the ingredients together,
cover and chill for 1 to 2 hours before
serving.
Serves 4

Raita

100 g (3½ oz)
   cucumber, thinly
   sliced
salt
2 × 150 g (5.2 oz)
   cartons natural
   yogurt
50 g (2 oz) spring
   onions, thinly
   sliced
1 green chilli*, seeded
   and finely chopped
coriander leaves*, to
   garnish

Place the cucumber in a colander, sprinkle with salt and leave to drain for 30 minutes. Dry thoroughly.

Mix the yogurt with salt to taste and fold in the cucumber, spring onion and chilli. Arrange in a serving dish and chill until required. Garnish with coriander leaves to serve.

Serves 4

NOTE: Raita can be made with other vegetables and with fruit – bananas are particularly good.

Cachumber

1 onion, chopped
250 g (8 oz)
    tomatoes, skinned
    and chopped
1-2 green chillies*,
    chopped
1-2 tablespoons
    vinegar
salt

Put the onion, tomatoes and chillies in a dish. Pour over the vinegar (the mixture must not be too liquid) and add salt to taste. Chill before serving.
Serves 4

Mango Chutney

1 kg (2 lb) very firm
    mangoes
500 g (1 lb) sugar
600 ml (1 pint)
    vinegar
5 cm (2 inch) piece
    ginger*
4 cloves garlic
½-1 tablespoon chilli
    powder*
1 tablespoon mustard
    seeds*
2 tablespoons salt
125 g (4 oz) raisins
    or sultanas

Peel the mangoes and cut into small pieces; set aside.

Place the sugar and all but 1 tablespoon of the vinegar in a pan and simmer for 10 minutes.

Place the ginger, garlic and remaining vinegar in an electric blender or food processor and work to a paste. Add to the pan and cook for 10 minutes, stirring.

Add the mango and remaining ingredients and cook, uncovered, for about 25 minutes, stirring as the chutney thickens.

Pour into hot sterilized jars, cover with waxed discs, then seal with cellophane covers and label. The chutney will keep for several months.
Makes about 1.25 kg (2½ lb)

86

Zalata

250 g (8 oz) ridge
   cucumbers, peeled
   and sliced
salt
1 green chilli*, sliced
1 tablespoon finely
   chopped coriander*
2 tablespoons vinegar
½ teaspoon sugar

Place the cucumber in a colander, sprinkle with salt and leave to drain for 30 minutes. Dry thoroughly. Place in a serving dish and add the remaining ingredients and 1 teaspoon salt. Mix well and chill thoroughly before serving.

Alternatively, place the drained cucumber in an electric blender or food processor with the whole chilli, coriander leaves, sugar and salt. Add 1 clove garlic and just ½ tablespoon vinegar and work to a smooth paste. Chill thoroughly before serving.
Serves 4

Coriander Chutney

25 g (1 oz) desiccated
   coconut
1 × 150 g (5.2 oz)
   carton natural
   yogurt
100 g (3½ oz)
   coriander*, including
   some fine stalks
2 green chillies*
juice of 1 lemon
1 teaspoon salt
1 teaspoon sugar

Mix the coconut with the yogurt and leave to stand for 1 hour. Place in an electric blender or food processor with the remaining ingredients and work until smooth. Chill before serving.
Serves 4

Prawn Relish

2 tablespoons oil
1 onion, chopped
4 dried red chillies*
2 green chillies*,
   chopped
½ teaspoon cumin
   seeds*
½ teaspoon turmeric*
1 clove garlic, crushed
2.5 cm (1 inch) piece
   ginger*, chopped
4 curry leaves*,
   crumbled
150 g (5 oz) prawns
1 tablespoon vinegar
salt

Heat the oil in a pan, add the onion and fry until golden. Crumble in the dried chillies. Add the fresh chillies, cumin, turmeric, garlic, ginger and curry leaves and fry for 2 minutes. Add the prawns and fry for 2 minutes.
   Add the vinegar and salt to taste and simmer, uncovered, for 3 to 4 minutes, until most of the liquid has evaporated. Serve hot or cold.
Serves 4

Date and Tomato Chutney

250 g (8 oz) dates,
   stoned and chopped
1 × 539 g (1 lb 3 oz)
   can tomatoes
1 onion, chopped
3.5 cm (1½ inch)
   piece ginger*,
   chopped
1 teaspoon chilli
   powder*
1 teaspoon salt
6 tablespoons vinegar

Put all the ingredients in a saucepan and stir well. Bring to the boil, then simmer, uncovered, for about 45 minutes, stirring occasionally, until thick. Serve cold.
Serves 4 to 6
NOTE: Extra chilli powder and salt may be added if wished, according to taste.

DESSERTS & SWEET MEATS

Semolina Barfi

50 g (2 oz) fine
  semolina
125 g (4 oz) sugar
450 ml (¾ pint)
  milk
50 g (2 oz) butter
10 cardamom*,
  peeled and crushed
75 g (3 oz) blanched
  almonds, halved
  and toasted

Place the semolina and sugar in a
heavy-based pan and stir in the milk
gradually until smooth. Add the
butter in small pieces. Bring to the
boil, stirring, then simmer for 3 to
4 minutes, until thickened, stirring
occasionally to prevent sticking. Add
the cardamom and continue cooking
for another 10 minutes until the
mixture leaves the side of the pan.

Spread on a buttered plate or dish
to a thickness of 1 to 1.5 cm (½ to
1 inch). Leave until almost cold, then
decorate with the almonds.

Serve cold, cut into slices or
squares.
Serves 4 to 6

Kheer

75 g (3 oz) long-grain rice
1.75 litres (3 pints) milk
50 g (2 oz) sultanas (optional)
caster sugar to taste
142 ml (5 fl oz) single cream
flaked almonds or lightly crushed cardamom seeds* to decorate

Place the rice and 1 litre (1¾ pints) of the milk in a heavy-based pan. Cook gently at simmering point for 45 minutes to 1 hour, until most of the milk has been absorbed.

Add the remaining milk and the sultanas, if using, stir well and continue simmering until thickened. Remove from the heat and add sugar to taste.

Leave until completely cold, stirring occasionally to prevent a skin forming, then stir in the cream.

Turn into small dishes and serve cold, sprinkled with flaked almonds or crushed cardamom seeds.

Serves 4

Almond Barfi

750 ml (1¼ pints)
    milk
50 g (2 oz) caster
    sugar
50 g (2 oz) ground
    almonds
6 cardamom*, peeled
    and crushed

Reduce the milk as for Mawa (see page 93).

When it is thick and lumpy, stir in the sugar, then add the almonds and cook for 2 minutes. Spread on a buttered plate and sprinkle with the crushed cardamom. Serve warm, cut into wedges or diamond shapes.
Serves 4

Shrikand

1 kg (2.2 lb) natural
    yogurt
1 packet powdered
    saffron
about 2 tablespoons
    caster sugar
about 1 tablespoon
    rose water
TO DECORATE:
1-2 teaspoons
    cardamom seeds*,
    crushed
1 tablespoon pistachio
    nuts, shelled and
    chopped

Turn the yogurt into a strainer lined with muslin and leave to drip over a bowl for 6 hours. Put the dried curds – there will be about 300 g (10 oz) – into a bowl and beat in the saffron. Add the sugar and taste; add a little more if you like, but it should not be too sweet. Mix in the rose water, a little at a time, until the mixture resembles thick cream. Cover and chill until required.

Spoon into individual bowls and decorate with the cardamom and pistachio nuts to serve.
Serves 4

Mawa

1.75 litres (3 pints) milk 3-4 tablespoons caster sugar	Cook the milk in a large, heavy–based saucepan for about 45 minutes, until it is reduced to a thick lumpy consistency. Stir occasionally and be careful not to let the milk burn. Add the sugar and continue cooking for 10 minutes. Spread the mixture on a lightly buttered plate: it should be a light cream coloured, softly–set toffee. Cut into wedges and serve cold. **Serves 4 to 6**

Carrot Halva

1.2 litres (2 pints) milk 250 g (8 oz) carrot, finely grated 75 g (3 oz) butter 1 tablespoon golden syrup 125 g (4 oz) sugar 50 g (2 oz) sultanas or raisins 1 teaspoon cardamom seeds*, crushed, to decorate	Place the milk and carrots in a heavy–based saucepan and cook over high heat, stirring occasionally, until the liquid has evaporated. Add the butter, syrup, sugar and fruit. Stir until the butter and sugar have melted, then cook for 15 to 20 minutes, stirring frequently, until the mixture starts to leave the side of the pan. Pour into a shallow buttered dish and spread evenly. Sprinkle with crushed cardamom. Cut into slices and serve warm or cold. **Serves 4 to 6**

93

INDEX

DRY

DRY

Non-alcoholic Cocktails, Cordials and Clever Concoctions

Clare Liardet

BANTAM PRESS

LONDON · NEW YORK · TORONTO · SYDNEY · AUCKLAND

Contents

Introduction

Whether you're the designated driver, teetotal, pregnant, having a go at Dry January, trying to lose weight or just cutting down, most of us will want a break from alcohol at some point. And an alcohol-free period is a brilliant opportunity to go wild with adventurous and delicious drinks.

More ingredients than ever before are available to experiment with: there are alcohol-free brewers around every corner, non-alcoholic spirits, and even new varieties of many classics like tonic water. A few of the recipes in this book need a little forethought and some do include the odd unfamiliar ingredient, but most can be knocked up with what you're likely to have to hand in the kitchen or garden.

Dry has plenty of inspiring examples of imaginative, grown-up, non-alcoholic alternatives, and there's definitely something for everyone. So whether you're planning a Friday night in with friends, a lazy Sunday brunch or a barbecue in the summer sun, you can find your dry drinks here.

Equipment

THE BASICS

Shaker

If you choose to invest in one piece of equipment, this is where I'd recommend you spend your money. I prefer a two-piece, all-metal shaker, as not only is it handy for packing into a basket for outings, it chills the drink quickly and with less dilution than ice. However, if you don't own one, a large jam jar will do!

Strainer

Many of these recipes require a strainer and a Hawthorne-style strainer is particularly useful. Make sure it's well made and that it's not loose where the handle meets the circle of the strainer. Alternatively, you could use a small fine-mesh sieve or a slotted spoon.

Muddler

This is a long pestle for crushing the oils out of zest or leaves, and mixing in sugar. They come in a variety of materials but wood is preferable as it does a gentler job than metal – even the end of a small rolling pin or wooden spoon would do.

Barspoon

This is a fun piece of equipment to have but certainly not essential. It's a very long-handled teaspoon, but a chopstick will do.

Squeezer

Fresh juice always makes such a difference in a dry drink, so I'd highly recommend investing in a squeezer. I love a hinged, stainless-steel press. They're easy to use with limes, lemons and oranges, and release the citrus oils too.

Knife, chopping board and peeler

You'll use a small, sharp knife and a handy chopping board all the time with these recipes. Just make sure that your knife is super sharp. I prefer using a Y-peeler, as it can also make lovely wide ribbons of whatever you need.

Measure or jigger

At home you don't need a strict bar measure, but it's useful to have to hand something that's consistent. I use a small, glass measuring cup that has both fluid ounces and millilitres marked on the side. Tablespoon and teaspoon measures are handy to have too.

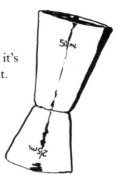

Juicer

If you're going to be experimenting with and exploring juices, a centrifugal juicer is a perfectly adequate and not-too-expensive piece of equipment. From experience, I'd recommend finding one that's easy to take apart to clean.

Blender

A blender of some sort is really useful – it could be a jug, NutriBullet or hand-held stick. I recently splashed out on a really powerful one and haven't looked back. It can whip up a frozen drink, crush ice or coffee beans, and make nut milk with ease, plus it's also fabulous for soup-making.

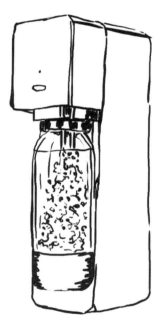

SodaStream

If you like making sparkling drinks, this machine can save you a lot of time and money in the long run. The end result doesn't necessarily replace a good-quality sparkling mineral water, but it can add instant fizz to any drink.

Glass jug for mixing or serving

A medium-size, thick glass jug, which can hold the right amount of ice, is all you need. A handle will ensure the drink stays as cool as possible.

Kilner jars, jam jars and bottles

These are great for storing sugar syrups or shrubs. You'll need to sterilize them before use and there are two main ways of doing this:

1. **The Oven Method.** Preheat the oven to 140°C/120°C fan/ gas mark 1. Wash the jars in hot, soapy water, and then rinse them well. Place the jars on a baking sheet and put them in the oven to dry completely. This will take about 15 minutes. If you're using Kilner jars, sterilize the rubber seals separately, in a pan of boiling water for a few minutes, as dry heat from the oven will damage them.

2. **The Dishwasher Method.** Fill your dishwasher with clean jars and run it on the hottest setting, or a steam setting if it has one. Once the cycle has finished, leave the jars to cool in the dishwasher.

GLASSES

The world is your oyster here, and I encourage you to have fun. You can spend a small fortune on traditional and beautiful glassware, but a French jam jar or a quirky, mismatched selection of glasses from a flea market can be just as fabulous. Heat-resistant glasses are fun, as unlike traditional mugs they allow the colour of the drink to show. I have a selection of different-sized, inexpensive Duralex ones.

In a traditional cocktail, the shape of a glass has a role to play in the way the drink is served. A few classic shapes are listed below.

1. **Highball** – narrow and thin, this holds fizz well
2. **Sling** – elegant, tapering at the bottom
3. **Tumbler** – short and heavy-bottomed
4. **Martini or cocktail** – small and delicate V-shaped cup on a stem
5. **Flute** – narrow and elegant on a stem, this holds fizz well
6. **Coupette, sour or daisy** – larger open cup on a stem

①   ②   ③

(4)   (5)   (6)

Ingredients

On the pages that follow is a collection of staples that I try to have in my kitchen at all times. None of them is difficult to find – you should be able to pick them up from a supermarket or buy them online.

FRUIT AND VEGETABLES

I'd urge you to use organic fruit and vegetables whenever possible, and if you're using the peel of citrus fruits try to find unwaxed varieties as wax will inhibit the release of oils. I think it's essential to have plenty of lemons and limes in the kitchen, and it's important to make sure you taste any seasonal fruits before you start preparing your drinks, as their sweetness can vary.

BITTERS

Bitters typically contain around 47% alcohol by volume, but you will only ever use a few drops at a time. They add complexity and depth to the flavour of a drink and, although it can be a little time-consuming to do so, it's very easy to make your own.

CELERY SALT

Simply made by mixing equal quantities of salt and ground celery seeds, it's easy to whip up fresh celery salt at home.

FRESH GINGER

A fiery rhizome or root, which has antibacterial, anti-inflammatory and antiviral properties.

JASMINE TEA FLOWERS

Green tea leaves are wrapped around a jasmine flower to form a ball which, when steeped in hot water, unfurls to reveal the flower within. They can be used to make a delicately flavoured and lightly scented tea.

KOMBUCHA

An ancient fermented tea made using a SCOBY (Symbiotic Culture of Bacteria and Yeast). It's full of probiotic cultures and, once brewed, is said to be great for the immune and digestive systems. There are many different flavours available in shops.

HIMALAYAN SALT

Mined in the Punjab region of Pakistan, this salt has a wonderful rose colour and is said to contain many minerals and trace minerals.

RAW HONEY

Raw honey hasn't been heated to high temperatures and so retains its beneficial nutrients. It's been used by different cultures for hundreds of years for its medicinal properties. Try to buy local, untreated honey if possible.

ROSEWATER

Not to be confused with the more concentrated rose essence, rosewater is made by steeping rose petals in water, and has been used for centuries as a flavouring.

TAMARIND

This bean-like fruit pod from the tamarind tree contains pulp and many seeds. It's used extensively in Southeast Asian cooking and tastes a little like a tart, lemony date. Interestingly, it's a key ingredient in both Worcestershire and HP sauce.

TURMERIC

This rhizome looks like a slimmer version of ginger but is a bright yellow-orange and can help clear infections and reduce inflammation in the body. Try to find fresh turmeric but, if you can't, the powder is great too.

SMALL BOTTLES OF GOOD-QUALITY MIXERS

A selection of ginger ale, ginger beer and tonic is essential. Some personal favourites are listed at the end of this section on page 25.

I've also included just a couple of lesser-known ingredients in these recipes. They might not be in your supermarket, but they can be found online or in health food shops.

MONTMORENCY CHERRY CONCENTRATE

A nutritious, tart cherry juice rich in phenolic acids.

SICHUAN (OR SZECHUAN) PEPPERCORNS

These originate from the Sichuan province of China and are not
actually pepper, but the dried berries of a type of ash tree. They have a
warm, spicy, citrusy aroma.

Don't Forget

Herbs and spices have been used for medicinal purposes for centuries,
so if you're pregnant or on medication it's worth checking which, if
any, you should avoid. *Jekka's Complete Herb Book* is my garden bible,
but do check with your doctor. Also be careful with grapefruit juice,
which affects the way your body metabolizes certain medications.

GARNISHES

Citrus

Make lengths of peel using a Y-peeler and twist them over the rim of
the glass to release the essential oils, which will then float on the surface
of the drink. Alternatively, you can use wedges or wheel-shaped slices.

Herbs

Use fresh herbs and try to avoid tearing or bruising the leaves. Whack
them gently on a hard surface to release their aroma and flavour before
putting them in a glass.

Edible flowers

My favourites are roses, violets, elderflowers, white and blue borage, and lavender.

Scented geranium leaves have been used for hundreds of years to add wonderful flavour but, like the bay leaf, aren't pleasant to actually eat.

ICE

You'll need lots of ice, so make sure you have space in the freezer. The more ice you put in a shaker, the quicker the drink will chill and the more it will dilute. Equally, the larger the ice cube the less dilution there will be.

Shapes

Be imaginative! Use silicon moulds or a plastic tub if you need a large block of ice for a jug. Alternatively, snipping the dividers out of a silicon ice-cube tray (carefully, with a pair of scissors) will give you long blocks. To make crushed ice, put some cubes in a clean cloth, tie the four corners together and smash against a solid surface.

Flavours

Think about freezing leftover juices, watermelon slices or halved lemons. These can be very useful when cooling a large jug, as too much melting ice will dilute the flavour of the drink.

Flowers and leaves

Freezing a flower or a few leaves in an ice cube can make a great visual addition to a drink. I particularly like using blue borage flowers, or celery leaves for savoury tipples.

Flavoured Waters

It's so simple and easy to have a jug of chilled, flavoured water on a table. I like to add:

- Cucumber, apple and tarragon
- Peach, raspberry, pomegranate and mint
- Strawberry and melon
- Mixed citrus fruits with mint

If you're organized, you can make a large jug the day before you need it and leave it to infuse overnight. Just add ice and extra water before serving.

A Note on Sugar

We all know that processed white sugar is best avoided, and thankfully there are some great alternatives available these days. While clear sugar syrup requires white sugar (and this is definitely worth doing for special occasions!), you can also use unrefined caster sugar. The syrup will look slightly coloured, but will still taste great.

Here are a few other alternatives:

Stevia A natural sweetener, about 300 times sweeter than sugar, from the *Stevia rebaudiana* plant. To me it has a faintly chocolatey taste.

Brown rice syrup Made from fermented cooked rice and complex carbohydrates.

Maple syrup A unique taste which is great added to Hot Buttered Spiced Apple (see page 111) if your apples are a bit tart.

SYRUPS AND SHRUBS

Sugar syrups are easy to make and will happily keep in the fridge for a week or two. I tend to make small batches and store them in sterilized and labelled jam jars or bottles. They give an unusual depth and layer of flavour to drinks, particularly those that are alcohol-free. Shrubs are an alternative to fruit cordials and are also easy to make at home. The word 'shrub' originates from the Arabic 'sharbah', which means 'drink'.

Simple Herb or Flower Syrup

The intensity of a herb's flavour varies throughout the year, so you might need to experiment with these lovely syrups. Just use a teaspoon to test the strength as it simmers, and adjust as necessary.

MAKES A 400ML BOTTLE

200g sugar

200ml water

herb/flower of choice, for example:

a few good sprigs of mint

2-3 tbsp lavender buds

12 lemon verbena leaves

2 sprigs of rosemary

a sprig of rose-scented geranium leaves

a dried hibiscus flower

Put the sugar and water in a pan on a low heat, stirring constantly, until the sugar dissolves. Bring the syrup to a simmer, add your chosen herb or flower and then continue to simmer for a further 5–10 minutes. Remove from the heat and allow to cool. Strain the syrup into a sterilized bottle.

Rhubarb Syrup

MAKES A 700ML BOTTLE

500g rhubarb, trimmed of leaves and roughly chopped

200ml water

350g sugar

Put the rhubarb in a pan with the water. Bring to the boil and then simmer until the rhubarb has almost completely broken down. This should take around 30 minutes.

Strain the cooked rhubarb through a clean piece of muslin (this will take a few hours), collecting the liquid in a bowl beneath.

Add the strained liquid to a clean pan with the sugar and bring to a simmer. Once the sugar has dissolved, leave to cool before transferring to a sterilized bottle.

When you're happy making the basic syrup, you can experiment a little. Perhaps add four strips of orange peel to the rhubarb in the pan, or 8–10 whole star anise for a spicier edge. If you want a sharper flavour, add the juice of three lemons when you add the sugar.

Smoky Lapsang Syrup

MAKES A 500ML BOTTLE

250ml water

2 Lapsang Souchong tea bags

250g sugar

In a pan, bring the water to a boil and add the tea bags. Take off the heat and leave to steep for 15 minutes. Once cool, remove the tea bags and add the sugar. Stir gently over a low heat until the sugar has dissolved, then bring to a simmer. Leave to cool again before transferring to a sterilized bottle. This is an intense-flavoured syrup so take care how much you add to your drinks!

Ginger and Black Peppercorn Syrup

MAKES AN 800ML BOTTLE

250g fresh, unpeeled ginger, chopped into small pieces

1 tbsp coarsely crushed peppercorns

1 litre water

400g sugar

a pinch of sea salt

Place the ginger, peppercorns, water, sugar and salt in a pan. Bring to the boil, then reduce the heat to a steady simmer for 45 minutes. Allow to cool, then strain the syrup through a fine-mesh strainer into a sterilized bottle.

Blackcurrant or Berry Shrub

MAKES A 300ML BOTTLE

2 heaped tbsp set honey

125ml organic apple cider vinegar

500g blackcurrants, or a 500g bag of frozen berries of your choice

In a pan, warm the honey with the vinegar so that the honey melts but doesn't boil. Place your fruit in a sterilized 500ml jar, then add the honeyed vinegar so that it just covers the fruit. Crush to mix using the end of a rolling pin, then put the lid on the jar and shake well. Leave somewhere cool for 3–4 days (or longer if you put it in the fridge), and shake once a day. Strain through a jelly bag or clean muslin set over a bowl, allowing the juice to drip through overnight. Then, using a funnel, decant the juice into a sterilized bottle. It can be stored in the fridge for a month and used like a cordial.

Chilli-infused Syrup

MAKES A 400ML BOTTLE

200ml water

200g sugar

4 red chillies, sliced in half lengthways

Add all the ingredients to a pan and bring to the boil. Allow them to bubble for 5 minutes until thickened slightly. Remove from the heat and set aside to cool. Pour into a sterilized jar or bottle.

Spice Syrup

MAKES A 750ML BOTTLE

250ml water

½ cinnamon stick

1 tsp black peppercorns

2 green cardamom pods

a pinch of grated nutmeg

10 coriander seeds

1 star anise

5cm fresh ginger, chopped

500g sugar

a strip of orange peel

Put the water in a pan and bring to the boil. Bash the spices in a pestle and mortar and add them to the boiling water with the ginger, sugar and the orange peel. Stir and remove from the heat. The longer you leave the spices to infuse, the more intense the syrup will be. I would recommend a minimum of 1 hour. Allow to cool, then strain through a fine-mesh sieve into a sterilized bottle.

Hibiscus Syrup

MAKES A 600ML BOTTLE

500ml water

90g white sugar

35g light brown sugar

12g dried hibiscus flowers

zest of 1 lemon

Add all the ingredients to a pan and bring to the boil. Reduce the heat and allow to simmer until the sugars dissolve and the flowers soften. This should take about 10 minutes. Remove from the heat and steep the syrup for around 5 minutes until the flavours combine. Strain the syrup into a sterilized bottle through a fine-mesh sieve. Press any solid ingredients with the back of a spoon to extract as much liquid as possible before discarding.

MY FAVOURITE QUICK FIXES

There's a growing market of interesting, grown-up, blessedly non-sweet, alcohol-free drinks out there. Here are a few that I think are definitely worth having in the cupboard, ready to grab at the drop of a hat.

Crodino This is a delicious, bitter aperitif from the company behind Aperol and Campari.

San Pellegrino Sanbitter There are two different versions: Dry, which is clear, and Red, which looks like Campari.

Double Dutch Produced by Dutch twins Joyce and Raissa, these mixers are divine and I'd highly recommend the summery Cucumber & Watermelon flavour.

Teetotal G 'n' T These flavoured tonics from the Temperance Spirit Company are perfect with ice and a slice.

Seedlip Marketed as the world's first non-alcoholic distilled spirit, Seedlip are doing something unique. There's a range of flavours and you'll find Garden – a fresh and summery flavour – and Spice – which is more wintery – used in recipes in this book. They're delicious with tonic or when added to a cocktail, and they offer a depth and complexity that belies their lack of alcohol.

Fever-Tree Tonics Delicious either on their own or when used as a mixer. Experiment with different flavours and combinations. I particularly love their elderflower tonic water.

NEW STARTS

These are drinks with bright, clean flavours, perfect for new beginnings and setting new goals. Whether it's the start of the year or a moment for pausing and reflecting, there are options here to set you on your way, to get you out of the door, or to welcome you home.

Blood Orange Sunrise

FOR 2

You will need:
2 tumblers

ice cubes

100ml fresh pomegranate
juice

juice of 1½ blood oranges

juice of ½ a lime

½ tbsp honey

plain or sparkling water

2 twists of blood
orange peel and a few
pomegranate seeds to
garnish

Place a handful of ice cubes in each
tumbler and divide the fresh pomegranate
juice between the two tumblers. In a
small bowl, whisk together the blood
orange juice, lime juice and honey. Divide
the mixture from the bowl between the
glasses and top with a splash of sparkling
or plain water, a twist of blood orange
peel and a few pomegranate seeds.

FLAVOUR Blood oranges have a short
season (from late winter to early spring)
but their rich ruby juice is a must-try.
Slightly tarter than that of a normal
orange, it's full of anthocyanins, a family
of antioxidant pigments common to
many flowers and fruit, but uncommon in
citrus fruits. With a hit of pomegranate
juice, this is a great kick-start to your day.

ADAPT To make a longer drink for later
in the day, add 400ml ginger ale or ginger
beer.

Nimbopani

FOR 2

You will need:
2 tumblers, blender

the juice of 6 small
south-Asian lemons or
3 large lemons

4–5 tbsp caster sugar

1½ tsp sea salt

a sprig of mint,
or 6 mint leaves

ice cubes

Blend the lemon juice, sugar and salt together until frothy. Add the mint leaves and blend for a further 5 seconds. Serve over ice in a glass and garnish with mint leaves.

INSPIRATION For me, this drink tastes of India. I can almost smell the heat and hear the honking horns. On a very warm day when you're feeling dehydrated, there's nothing more refreshing than this intense little number. It's a fantastic pick-me-up after exercise too.

ADAPT For an equally delicious alternative, use six juicy limes instead of lemons.

Score per recipe? 3/10!

Very margharita like in taste. Too salty to drink if you follow the recipe so next time I'll salt the rim of the glass instead!

Tropical Morning Smoothie

FOR 2

You will need:
2 large, stemmed glasses, blender

½ large ripe pineapple, peeled, cored and cut into chunks

½ large ripe papaya, peeled, seeds removed

1 tsp vanilla extract

200ml full-fat coconut milk

juice of 1 lime

½ tsp ground turmeric

150ml coconut water or water

small piece of fresh ginger, peeled (optional)

ice cubes

Blend the pineapple, papaya flesh, vanilla extract, coconut milk, lime juice, turmeric, coconut water and ginger together until smooth and frothy. Add more water if necessary.

Pour over ice and enjoy straight away, or transfer to a Thermos to keep cool for later.

HEALTHY Refreshing, anti-inflammatory and full of antioxidants, this is a great smoothie to wake up to. Alternatively, it makes the perfect post-workout treat.

Raw Spicy Mary

FOR 1

You will need:
highball, juicer

3 ripe plum tomatoes

1 celery stick, trimmed

½ red pepper, seeds removed

½ red chilli, seeds removed

1 tsp raw or unpasteurized cider vinegar

juice of ½ a small lemon

1 tsp extra virgin olive oil

a large pinch of sea salt

a wedge of lemon

Himalayan salt, or another pinch of sea salt

ice cubes

freshly grated horseradish or freshly ground black pepper to garnish

celery stick to stir

Wash the tomatoes, celery, pepper and chilli, then push them through your juicer. Stir in the cider vinegar, lemon juice, olive oil and the large pinch of salt. Taste and adjust the flavours, if necessary. There should be a lovely balance of sweet, salty and spicy.

Stir well before pouring into your glass rimmed with lemon juice and Himalayan salt, and filled with ice cubes. Finish with a sprinkling of fresh horseradish or black pepper, and a celery stick to stir.

FLAVOUR This is a really fresh and aromatic take on a Virgin Mary. It's a feast for all the senses, from the heady scent of ripe tomatoes to the vibrant colour and sweet-hot tingle on the tongue. A true wake-up call.

Pineapple Mint Green

FOR 2

You will need:
2 highballs, blender

¼ large ripe pineapple, peeled, cored and cut into chunks

40g organic spinach

40g lettuce

1 ripe pear, peeled and pips removed

½ banana (if the pineapple isn't ripe enough)

1 tsp flaxseeds

10 mint leaves

juice of ½ a lime

ice cubes

Wash the pineapple, spinach and lettuce, and add them with the peeled pear to your blender. Check for sweetness and add the banana, if necessary. Add the flaxseeds and mint leaves, and blend thoroughly until smooth, then add lime juice to taste. Stir well and pour on top of the ice, or into a Thermos for a post-workout boost.

HEALTHY This is a lovely, fresh, fragrant green juice that's easy to make at the beginning of the day. It uses pear rather than apple, so isn't too sugary, and pineapple is a rich source of minerals, enzymes and vitamins. This is a powerhouse start to the day.

Made without Lettuce (thick milk shake consisty) (and no banana)
Score = ☀ 9/10 !

Fiery Ginger and Apple Boost

. . . .

FOR 1

You will need:
tumbler, juicer

2 small dessert apples, cored

50g fresh ginger, peeled

ice cubes

100ml sparkling water

1 tsp agave syrup (optional)

slice of apple to garnish

Chop the apples to fit the juicer, then add in the ginger and blend. Pour 150ml of the apple-and-ginger mix into a glass of ice, and top up with sparkling water. Stir in a little agave syrup to taste, if the apples are too tart. Garnish with a slice of apple.

FLAVOUR I love the taste of ginger in the morning and have a guilty love of ginger beer at any time of the day. This is an instant, healthy, fizzy ginger hit, with none of the vast amounts of sugar found in commercial brands of ginger beer. It's completely invigorating.

Ginger, Turmeric and Chilli Tea

FOR 2

You will need:
*2 heatproof glasses
or mugs, teapot*

1 tbsp fresh ginger,
peeled and finely grated

½ tsp ground turmeric

a tiny pinch of cayenne
pepper or a slice of red
chilli

¼ tsp black pepper (to aid
turmeric absorption)

600ml hot water

juice of ½ a lemon

a little raw honey

slices of fresh ginger
and lemon to garnish

Add the ginger to a teapot with the turmeric, cayenne and black pepper.

Fill with very hot (but not boiling) water, stir and then leave to steep for 10 minutes. If you like, strain the liquid before pouring into heatproof glasses or mugs, then stir in the lemon juice and honey. Garnish with a fresh slice of ginger and lemon.

HEALTHY This golden tea is a fabulous way to banish the winter blues and sniffles. The healing, immunity-boosting and anti-inflammatory properties of ginger and turmeric have been used for centuries. This is a bit of warm sunshine on a chilly grey day.

Kiwi and Cucumber Juice

FOR 1

You will need:
highball, blender

¼ large cucumber,
roughly chopped

1 kiwi fruit, peeled

½ pear, peeled and pips
removed

a handful of watercress

½ stick celery, trimmed
and roughly chopped

leaves from 2 sprigs
of mint

½ tbsp milled flaxseed

100ml coconut water

ice cubes

a slice of peeled kiwi fruit
to garnish

Blend the cucumber, kiwi, pear, watercress, celery, mint, flaxseed and coconut water until smooth, adding water if needed. Pour into a tall glass on top of a couple of ice cubes. Garnish with a slice of peeled kiwi.

FLAVOUR A refreshing green juice for the morning, with plenty of goodness and fibre. Watercress is a true superstar in the world of nutrition, and I love this peppery hit to start the day.

FRIDAY NIGHTS

After a busy week, I often need a
pick-me-up to start the weekend.
And whether it's an impromptu
gathering or a carefully planned
party, I like to have some delicious
ingredients in the fridge, ready to
create a little something for myself
or a recipe that can be scaled up
to water a group.

Blood Orange and Sage Margarita

- -

FOR 1

You will need:
chilled coupette, shaker, strainer

125ml blood orange juice

2 tbsp freshly squeezed lime juice

1 tbsp Hibiscus Syrup (see page 24)

3 sage leaves (reserve one to garnish)

ice cubes

a wedge of lime

Himalayan salt

Put the blood orange juice, lime juice, hibiscus syrup and two sage leaves in a shaker with ice, and shake until chilled. If you like a salt rim, run a wedge of lime around the rim of the chilled glass and dip it on to a saucer spread with salt. Strain the mixture into the glass and garnish with the third sage leaf.

FLAVOUR There is never a wrong time for a margarita in my book. The wonderful tart, salty tang of the drink is captured here and given depth with the hibiscus syrup. The sage provides an aromatic back note.

HEALTHY Blood oranges give the most beautiful juice, as well as being packed with antioxidants, so grab them in late winter or early spring when they're in season.

Blueberry Julep

. . . .

FOR 1

You will need:
*tumbler or copper mug,
muddler*

40g blueberries

6 mint leaves

½ a lime, cut into wedges

1 tsp sugar

crushed ice

200ml ginger beer

a sprig of mint and a
wedge of lime to garnish

In a large glass muddle the blueberries, six mint leaves, lime and sugar. Transfer to your tumbler or mug and add crushed ice, before pouring in the ginger beer and garnishing with the sprig of mint and wedge of lime.

FLAVOUR This may be a simple recipe but it ticks all the boxes. The refreshing lime cuts through the warmth of the ginger, while the blueberries give the drink a tart sweetness. Juleps were traditionally served in pewter or silver cups, and held by the base or the rim, which helped to keep the drink cold.

Kombucha Spritz

FOR 1

You will need:
highball, jug, muddler, strainer

2cm rhubarb, sliced

3 strips of orange peel

2 tsp Montmorency cherry concentrate

120ml fresh orange juice

3 tsp Simple Herb Syrup made with rosemary (see page 22)

ice cubes

a wedge of lime

150ml kombucha

a dash of Angostura Bitters (optional)

a twist of orange peel

trimmed rhubarb stick to stir

Place the sliced rhubarb in a jug with the orange peel and the cherry concentrate, and muddle to release the juice from the rhubarb. Add the orange juice and rosemary syrup, and muddle again.

Strain into a highball full of ice, then squeeze in a wedge of lime and top up with the kombucha. If you wish to use Angostura Bitters, add a dash now. Finish with a twist of orange peel dropped into the drink, and a stick of rhubarb to stir.

INSPIRATION Aperol Spritz makes me think of that delicious moment when the ski boots are off and everyone is gathered again, pink-cheeked, to talk about their day. I love the bitter notes in cocktails and was fascinated to read that Aperol lists rhubarb amongst its many ingredients. I think this many-layered drink belongs in the same family.

FLAVOUR You may already be familiar with kombucha, a fermented tea made by combining bacteria, yeast and sugar. It has a tart, sweet flavour, and you can either make your own or buy it ready-made.

Ginger, Lime and Angostura Fizz

FOR 1

You will need:
tumbler

30ml Ginger and Black Peppercorn Syrup (see page 23)

juice of ½ a lime

ice cubes

sparkling water

a few dashes of Angostura Bitters

slices or wedges of lime to garnish

Pour the ginger syrup into a tumbler and add the lime juice. Half fill the glass with ice and top up with sparkling water. Shake in a few dashes of Angostura Bitters, stir and add the slices or wedges of lime to garnish.

FLAVOUR This is a classic. It's simple and delicious yet often overlooked. You can use bottled ginger beer instead of the syrup (although you may need more sparkling water to counteract the sweetness) but in my eyes the heat of the cordial makes it extra special.

Raspberry and Lavender Shrub

FOR 1

You will need:
highball, muddler

2 sprigs of mint or lavender

25ml Berry Shrub made with raspberries (see page 23)

ice cubes

juice of 1 lime

1 tsp Simple Flower Syrup made with lavender (see page 22)

sparkling water

wedge of lime to garnish

Lightly bruise the mint or lavender sprigs with a muddler, then leave them in the raspberry shrub for half an hour.

Half fill a tall glass with ice. Remove the sprigs from the shrub and pour the shrub on to the ice. Add half of the lime juice to the glass, pour in the lavender syrup and top up with sparkling water. Garnish with a wedge of lime.

INSPIRATION I love that shrubs have a long history, dating as far back as the Babylonians, and feel like elegant, beautiful drinks. Here, lavender adds a woody, floral element while the raspberry shrub has an intensity and depth of flavour that is missing in a simple cordial.

Peach and Lemongrass Cup

. . . .

FOR 1

You will need:
tumbler, muddler, jug

½ stalk lemongrass, cut in half lengthways

a large sprig of mint

1 ripe peach, sliced into wedges

250ml cloudy apple juice

1 lemon, thinly sliced

ice cubes

sparkling water

a stalk of lemongrass to stir

Muddle the lemongrass and the sprig of mint in a jug. Add the peach, apple juice and lemon, and leave to stand for at least an hour. This will help the flavours to develop.

Half fill a tumbler with ice, pour in some juice and top up with sparkling water. Add a lemongrass stalk to use as a swizzle stick.

FLAVOUR This is a showstopper. It smells wonderful, and the woody, citrus notes of lemongrass stop it from becoming too sweet. This is one to make when the shops and markets are full of peaches, and you can come home with a whole boxful.

Totally Citrus Fizz

You will need:
tumbler, muddler

½ stalk lemongrass, outer
leaves removed, core
roughly chopped

ice cubes

30ml freshly squeezed
lime juice

15ml sugar syrup

sparkling water

lemongrass stalk to stir

Place the lemongrass in a tumbler and
muddle to release its oils. Fill the glass
with ice and pour in the lime juice and
sugar syrup. Top up with sparkling
water, stir briefly and garnish with the
remaining lemongrass stalk.

INSPIRATION This is a drink to revive
and restore. The aromatic lemongrass
always sends me back to Brazil where, as
happens in the tropics, night falls quickly.
There's no time for languishing, and this
tipple brings the senses back to life, ready
for a Friday night.

Seedlip Asparagus Tonic

FOR 1

You will need:
tumbler, Y-peeler, muddler

1 stalk asparagus

ice cubes

25ml freshly squeezed lime juice

10ml Simple Herb Syrup made with rosemary (see page 22)

50ml Seedlip Garden 108

tonic water

a wedge of lime

an asparagus spear to garnish

Using a Y-peeler, shear the stalk of asparagus lengthways until you have a few shavings. Place these in the tumbler and press gently with a muddler.

Half fill your tumbler with ice and pour in the lime juice, rosemary syrup and Seedlip Garden. Stir gently to mix, then top up with tonic water. Squeeze the wedge of lime over the top, and garnish with the asparagus spear.

INSPIRATION Right when the day is softening into evening, I love sitting in the garden for a moment. It's the perfect time to sip something delicious before cooking supper. This drink is green, fresh and aromatic – just the thing to lift the fatigue of a long week.

LAZY SUNDAYS

Sunday brunch heralds a slower pace, a pause in the hectic modern week. It should feed all the senses, from the crisp opening of a newspaper to the aroma of freshly brewed coffee. Lazy limbs are roused slowly and taste buds can be woken with an array of flavours.

Bloody Heifer

FOR 1

You will need:
highball, shaker

125ml tomato juice

125ml beef bouillon (or home-made beef stock)

½ tsp freshly grated horseradish

2 dashes of Worcestershire sauce

3 dashes of Tabasco sauce

a pinch of freshly ground pepper

15ml freshly squeezed lemon juice

a pinch of celery salt

ice cubes

wedges of lemon and lime to garnish

celery stick to stir

Add the tomato juice, beef bouillon, horseradish, Worcestershire sauce, Tabasco sauce, pepper, lemon juice and celery salt to a shaker containing ice, and roll it gently to mix the ingredients.

Pour into a highball glass and garnish with a wedge of lemon and lime, and a tender celery stick.

ADAPT This is a super-tasty version of a Virgin Mary – it's almost a liquid lunch. I recommend transferring it to a Thermos and taking it on a morning stomp in the countryside to revive you halfway. If you do use a Thermos, chill the Bloody Heifer beforehand and don't use ice as the drink will become too diluted.

Chilli and Lime Margarita

FOR 1

You will need:
tumbler, large jug

150ml freshly squeezed lime juice

50ml Chilli-infused Syrup (see page 23)

25ml fresh orange juice

3 limes, thinly sliced

fine sea salt

wedge of lime

crushed ice

slices of lime to garnish

Combine the lime juice, chilli syrup, orange juice and sliced limes in a large jug and allow to stand for 10 minutes.

Pour some salt on to a plate, slide the wedge of lime around the rim of your glass and then dip the glass in the salt. Fill with the margarita and ice, and serve garnished with slices of lime.

INSPIRATION I first tasted chilli and lime margaritas with my family at a beach bar in Noosa, Australia. It was after a long flight and I've been in love with them ever since. This recipe is a take on that fabulous drink and I think it hits the spot, whether you're by the seaside or at home on a Sunday morning.

Beetroot Virgin Mary

FOR 2

You will need:
large jug and 2 tall glasses, juicer

800g smallish beetroots, scrubbed, topped, tailed and roughly chopped, or 500ml shop-bought beetroot juice

juice of 2 limes (reserve the juiced halves)

1 tsp Tabasco sauce

1 tsp Worcestershire sauce

1 tsp celery salt

sea salt and freshly ground black pepper

ice cubes

freshly grated horseradish to garnish (you can keep this ready-peeled in the freezer or can grate from frozen using a Microplane grater)

2 celery sticks to stir

Juice the beetroots, if not using shop-bought juice, and set aside. It's worth noting that small beetroots tend to have a milder flavour.

Mix the lime juice, Tabasco and Worcestershire sauces, and the celery salt together in a large jug, add the beetroot juice and put it in the fridge to cool.

If you like, rub the juiced lime halves around the rims of the tall glasses, then dip the rims into a saucer containing the salt and freshly ground pepper. Otherwise, simply fill the glasses with ice and top up with the beetroot juice. Add some freshly grated horseradish and serve with a celery stick.

HEALTHY This is a healthier version of the classic Bloody Mary, using beetroot juice as the base, which is very easy to make yourself if you have a juicer. If your beetroot is organic, there's no need to peel it in advance. This nutrient-rich juice is earthy and sweet, but be mindful that beetroots have the highest sugar content of any vegetable.

Strawberry Booster

FOR 1

You will need:
small tumbler, blender

1 heaped tbsp raw honey

juice of 1 large lemon

a pinch of sea salt

50ml hot water

small handful ripe
strawberries, hulled
(smaller berries tend to
taste better)

6 mint leaves

a splash of good-quality
balsamic vinegar

ice cubes

chilled water, still or
sparkling

a sprig of mint to garnish

Put the honey, lemon juice, salt and hot water into a blender. Blend carefully for a few seconds, then add the strawberries and pulse the mixture until it's lovely and frothy. Add the mint leaves and a splash of balsamic vinegar before blending again for a further 5 seconds.

Pour the drink over ice and top with chilled water, either still or sparkling, and garnish with a sprig of mint.

FLAVOUR This delicious strawberry drink is the perfect antidote to that morning-after feeling, or it's the ideal post-workout tonic. The addition of the salt, balsamic vinegar and lemon makes the fruit taste richer and sweeter.

Paloma Fizz

FOR 1

You will need:
tumbler

60ml pink grapefruit juice

a pinch of Himalayan salt or sea salt

2 tbsp Simple Herb Syrup made with rosemary (see page 22)

crushed ice

150ml sparkling water or grapefruit soda

a sprig of rosemary to garnish

Pour the grapefruit juice into the tumbler and stir in the pinch of salt and rosemary syrup. Fill the glass with ice and then top up with sparkling water. Garnish with the sprig of rosemary.

FLAVOUR Grapefruit, high in vitamin C and potassium, is a great way to start the day, and pink grapefruit has the added benefit of being rich in beta-carotene. This is a pretty, colourful and refreshing drink with a hint of savoury rosemary. It takes a simple glass of morning grapefruit juice to a brand-new level.

Watermelon Mary

FOR 4

You will need:
4 tall glasses, blender

½ small watermelon, skinned

1kg ripe tomatoes, peeled, or 500ml good-quality tomato juice

1 red pepper, deseeded

1 garlic clove, peeled and chopped

a pinch of sea salt

75ml raw cider vinegar

100ml olive oil

ice cubes

seeds of a passion fruit to garnish

Blend the watermelon, tomatoes, red pepper, garlic and salt together, then add the vinegar and olive oil slowly.

Half fill a glass with ice and pour in a serving of juice. Top with passion fruit seeds. If making a jug, chill in the fridge for several hours before serving.

INSPIRATION I was first given a bowl of refreshing watermelon gazpacho on a hot sunny day in Portugal. It was made from a recipe from a Colombian friend and it completely surpassed the straightforward tomato version I was used to. This version is a great what's-the-secret-ingredient drink – people rarely guess watermelon!

Iced Cardamom Coffee

FOR 2

You will need:
2 tumblers, coffee grinder or powerful blender, pestle and mortar, Kilner or large lidded receptacle, fine-mesh sieve, clean piece of muslin

100g coarse-grind roasted coffee, or 8 tbsp ready-ground coffee

8 green cardamom pods

1 litre cold water (the ratio of coffee to water should be 1:8, so increase the quantities accordingly if you need more)

ice cubes

milk, cream or sugar syrup

If freshly grinding your coffee beans, set your grinder to its most coarse setting. You're looking for coffee grounds the same consistency as breadcrumbs. If you don't have a grinder, use a powerful blender.

Pound the cardamom pods with a pestle and mortar, then discard the skin of the pods before crushing the seeds lightly.

Sterilize a large Kilner jar (or any large receptacle with a lid) and place your cardamom and ground coffee in the bottom of the jar. Cover with the cold water, stir well, then close the lid and leave the mixture for 18–24 hours, either in or out of the fridge.

Strain the mixture through a fine-mesh sieve over a large bowl, then repeat two or three times through a clean piece of muslin or a few sheets of paper towel until the coffee is clear. If it stays a bit murky it simply means your grind was too fine.

Pour over ice and, if you like, add cold milk, cream or whipped cream. With or without a touch of sugar syrup, this is a wonderfully refreshing drink for a warm day.

ADAPT Cinnamon, hazelnut and vanilla are equally delicious in iced coffee, or you could add the Spice Syrup on page 24 instead of the sugar syrup.

Raw Rhubarb Spritz

. . . .

FOR 1

You will need:
tall glass

ice cubes

80ml sweetened raw
rhubarb juice (see recipe
below)

juice of ½ a lime

sparkling water

trimmed rhubarb stick
to stir

Fill your glass with several pieces of ice,
and pour in the rhubarb juice. Add the
lime juice and top with sparkling water.
Use a stick of rhubarb to stir.

FLAVOUR When the first pink stalks
of rhubarb start to push up through the
winter earth, I really feel spring is just
around the corner. This spritz tastes and
smells intensely of rhubarb, undiluted
by any cooking. Raw rhubarb – but on no
account the leaf, which is poisonous – is
delicious dipped in either sugar or salt.

For the sweetened raw rhubarb juice

You will need:
blender, fine-mesh sieve

approx. 1kg rhubarb,
trimmed of leaves and
cut into 1cm pieces

150g caster sugar

In a large bowl toss the rhubarb in the
sugar and cover with cling film. Leave in
the fridge for at least 6 hours or, ideally,
overnight.

Place the rhubarb into a blender along
with all the juice that has collected in
the bowl, and blitz for 1 minute. Push
the mixture through a fine-mesh sieve,
collecting the liquid from it in a bowl
beneath. Pour into a sterilized bottle.
It will keep in the fridge for a few days.

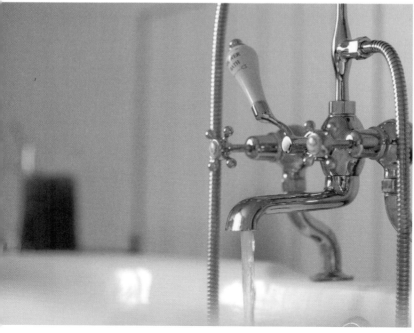

LONG SUMMERS

The high sun, long evenings and heady scents of summer are an invitation to laze around outside, sipping cool drinks with friends. Fruits are ripe, bees hum in the lavender, and a sweet-scented garden or park provides the perfect excuse to turn a quick drink into an impromptu gathering. All of these drinks are fragrant, cool and can be transformed easily from a single glass into a sociable jug.

Blackcurrant Shrub Summer Cup

FOR 1

You will need:
highball, muddler

a handful of mint or
lemon verbena leaves

ice cubes

40ml Blackcurrant Shrub
(see page 23)

1 tsp rosewater

150ml sparkling water

a curl of lemon peel,
some mint leaves and a
sprig of blackcurrants to
garnish

Lightly bruise the mint or lemon verbena
leaves by placing them in a glass and
squashing them with the muddler. Half
fill the glass with ice, then pour in the
shrub and add around a teaspoon of
rosewater to taste. You're aiming for a
light scent of summer roses, so go gently
and add more, drop by drop, if needed.
Top up with sparkling water.

Garnish your glass with some mint leaves
and a sprig of blackcurrants.

INSPIRATION This drink reminds me
of long summer days as a child, guzzling
icy Ribena. I remember being called
over, gulping down the sweet tang of
blackcurrant, then rushing back out to
play. This is a more grown-up version.

Passion Fruit and Lime Sparkler

FOR 1

You will need:
tumbler, muddler

½ a lime, cut into wedges

a good handful of mint leaves

1 tbsp caster sugar

2 slices of fresh ginger, peeled

2 passion fruits, cut in half (reserve one ½ to garnish)

ice cubes

sparkling water

a wedge of lime to garnish

Muddle the lime, mint leaves and sugar together in a glass. Add your two slices of ginger and the juice and seeds of three halves of passion fruit. Fill the glass with ice, add sparkling water and stir. Garnish with passion fruit seeds and a wedge of lime.

INSPIRATION Passion fruit is incredibly zesty and full of flavour. It always makes me think of hot countries and tropical days. So this passion fruit and lime sparkler was designed with summer in mind, and is a great way to cool down after a day in the sun.

Drivers' Pimm's Cup

FOR 4

You will need:
large jug and highballs, small jug

40ml black tea

½ tsp dark, soft brown sugar

40ml ginger beer (or 10ml Ginger and Black Peppercorn Syrup (see page 23) and 30ml soda water)

½ tsp good-quality balsamic vinegar

ice cubes

2 oranges, sliced

slices of cucumber

2 lemons, sliced

lemonade

borage flowers from the garden and sprigs of mint to garnish

Make a cup of strong black tea. Pour 40ml of the tea into a small jug, then stir in the sugar and leave to cool. Add the ginger beer and balsamic vinegar.

Fill your serving jug (or some chilled tall glasses) with ice cubes and the sliced fruit and cucumber. Add one part Drivers' Pimm's to three parts lemonade. Decorate with borage flowers and sprigs of mint.

INSPIRATION Pimm's was one of the first drinks I was ever given in my grandparents' garden, and it always reminds me of long, easy family lunches that drift lazily into the evening.

Cucumber and Elderflower Cooler

FOR 1

You will need:
highball, muddler

a handful of fresh basil

4 slices of cucumber

1 lime, cut into wedges

40ml elderflower cordial

20ml Simple Herb Syrup
made with rosemary
(see page 22)

a dash of freshly
squeezed lime juice

crushed ice

sparkling water

a sprig of basil and long
baton of cucumber to
garnish

Muddle the basil, cucumber and lime in a highball. Add the elderflower cordial, rosemary syrup and dash of lime juice. Half fill the glass with crushed ice, then top up with sparkling water. Stir everything together and garnish with a sprig of basil and a long baton of cucumber.

FLAVOUR This is a deliciously sophisticated drink with aromatic back notes of basil and rosemary. The cucumber gives the drink a clean, green freshness, which makes it the perfect aperitif.

ADAPT It's also wonderful made with fresh mint instead of basil.

Ginger Fever

FOR 4

You will need:
large jug and
4 tumblers, muddler

½ stalk lemongrass, cut lengthways

120ml Ginger and Black Peppercorn Syrup (see page 23)

juice of 2 limes

ice cubes

750ml ginger beer

4 strips of orange peel and 4 wedges of lime to garnish

a stalk of lemongrass sliced lengthways to use as swizzle stick

Lightly bash the lemongrass with a muddler and place it in a large jug. Pour in the ginger syrup and the lime juice, then half fill the jug with ice. Top it up with ginger beer.

Twist a strip of orange peel over each glass to release the oils before dropping it in. Divide the contents of the jug between the four glasses and serve each with a wedge of lime and a lemongrass swizzle stick.

INSPIRATION When he arrived home from work my father would always pour himself a gin and ginger beer. With the aromatic, bright citrus notes of lemongrass cutting through the warmth of the ginger, this simple, restorative drink signals the end of the day to me.

Still Rose Lemonade

FOR 4

You will need:
*large jug and
4 tumblers, heatproof
bowl*

4 large lemons, sliced

80g sugar

500ml boiling water

1–2 tsp rosewater to
taste, or a dash of Simple
Flower Syrup made with
rose-scented geranium
leaves (see page 22)

ice cubes

Put the lemons and sugar into a
heatproof bowl and cover them with the
boiling water. Stir until the sugar has
dissolved. Allow the liquid to cool, then
mix in the rosewater or rose-geranium
syrup a little at a time, tasting as you go.
It should be very lemony with just a hint
of rose. Fill a jug with ice and pour in the
lemonade ready to serve.

SERVING SUGGESTION The essence of
summer. Refreshing zesty lemons with a
hint of fragrant rose. This is a fabulous
drink to take on a picnic. Before you
set off, fill a large Thermos (or sealable
jug) with ice and pour in the lemonade.
By the time you arrive, the ice will have
melted, leaving a deliciously cool, thirst-
quenching treat.

Summer Storm

FOR 1

You will need:
*blender, shaker,
coupette*

100g ripe pineapple,
peeled, cored and cut
into chunks

25ml Ginger and Black
Peppercorn Syrup
(see page 23)

15ml organic egg white

ice cubes

1 small piece of stem
ginger

sparkling water

Blend the pineapple for about 30 seconds until it's crushed but not puréed. Mix 100ml of the pineapple with the ginger syrup and the egg white in a cocktail shaker. Add the ice cubes and shake again.

Put the stem ginger in your glass and pour in the cocktail. Top it up with a little sparkling water.

FLAVOUR The peppery ginger syrup cuts through the sweetness and enhances the tart, fragrant qualities of the pineapple. Just imagine sipping this sitting on a veranda, while warm tropical rain thunders on the roof.

Roasted Peach Lemonade

FOR 2

You will need:
*blender, pitcher and
2 coupettes*

4 medium peaches, sliced
in half and de-stoned

1 tbsp sugar

500ml home-made
lemonade (follow the
recipe for Still Rose
Lemonade on page 96
but omit the rosewater)

ice cubes

sparkling water

Preheat the oven to 200°C/180°C fan/
gas mark 6. Place the peaches skin side
down in a baking dish and sprinkle with
sugar. Roast for about 25 minutes, or
until the tops are juicy and the skins are
easy to pinch off.

Put the roasted, skinned peaches in a
blender and add enough lemonade to
cover them. Blitz until the peaches are
puréed completely and the liquid is a
little foamy and frothy. Pour the mixture
into a pitcher and stir in the rest of the
lemonade. Allow to cool and then, before
serving, add the ice and top up with a bit
of sparkling water.

FLAVOUR A perfectly ripe peach evokes
the scents of honey, rose and summer,
and roasting the fruit produces a warm
caramel flavour to enhance this summery
drink.

WOOD SMOKE WARMERS

As autumn begins, the light softens, fires are lit and we wrap up for walks to gather blackberries and crab apples. Fragrant quinces, apples and pears are ready to pick, and I find myself pausing while rambling to sip a delicious, spiced drink from a Thermos. Make the drinks in this chapter to have by a bonfire or for when you arrive home with cold-flushed cheeks and chilly hands.

Autumn Sangria

. . . .

FOR 2

You will need:
large jug, 2 large goblets

1 apple, thinly sliced (using a mandolin if possible)

½ small pear, thinly sliced (using a mandolin if possible)

1 red plum, sliced into wedges

½ small orange, sliced

a handful of cherries, fresh or frozen

150ml apple juice, chilled

75ml fresh orange juice

1 tsp Ginger and Black Peppercorn Syrup (see page 23)

ice cubes

tonic water

2 sprigs of mint to garnish

In a jug, combine all the fruit with the apple juice, orange juice and ginger syrup, then refrigerate for a couple of hours.

Once chilled, divide between two large goblets filled with ice, top up with tonic water and garnish with a sprig of mint.

FLAVOUR This recipe is just a guideline. It's a generous, bountiful drink and I particularly enjoy using a mixture of different apples to make it. If you have an apple tree in your garden, or access to one, use fresh apple juice. You could also juice apples from the supermarket. When the quantities are scaled up, this looks wonderful in a large jug, so throw in the fruits you gather and share it with friends.

Warming Dark Berry Shrub

FOR 1

You will need:
heatproof glass

150ml apple juice

a slice of lemon

2 bay leaves

50ml Berry Shrub made
with blackberries (see
page 23)

1 tbsp honey

bay leaf to garnish

Gently warm the apple juice in a pan
with the lemon slice and your two bay
leaves. Simmer over a low heat for 5
minutes to allow the flavours to infuse.
Do not let it boil. Add the blackberry
shrub and honey, and stir until dissolved.

Make sure the drink is warm enough,
then pour the liquid into a heatproof
glass and garnish with a bay leaf.

FLAVOUR For me, the pairing of tart,
deep-purple blackberries and sweet,
aromatic apple signals autumn. The
wonderful colour and scented steam of
this drink certainly keep the chilly wind
at bay.

Cranberry and Hibiscus Allspice

. . . .

FOR 1

You will need:
*heatproof glass,
strainer*

250ml cranberry juice

3 allspice berries

1 cinnamon stick

a slice of fresh ginger,
peeled

1 star anise

½ tsp Sichuan
peppercorns (or black
peppercorns)

1 bay leaf

a pinch of hibiscus petals
or a flower

25ml Hibiscus Syrup
(see page 24)

Add all the ingredients apart from the hibiscus syrup to a pan, then cover and simmer over a low heat for about 10 minutes. Add the hibiscus syrup and taste. You're looking for a balance between sweet and tart, with just a hint of spice.

Strain the liquid to remove the whole spices and bay leaf but put the hibiscus flower, cinnamon stick and ginger slice back into the strained liquid. Serve straight away in a heatproof glass or pour into a Thermos for later.

FLAVOUR The fragrant steam showcases the very best of autumn and winter spices, while the hibiscus gives an unusual and sharp lemony note.

ADAPT A welcoming warm, ruby, spiced drink to banish the darkening nights, this is particularly delicious when served with spiced biscuits for dunking. Crisp biscotti work especially well.

Hot Buttered Spiced Apple

FOR 1

You will need:
heatproof glass or mug

250ml cloudy apple juice

juice of ½ a lemon, plus
1 strip of zest

juice of ½ an orange, plus
1 strip of zest

½ cinnamon stick

1 whole clove

2 allspice berries

¼ tsp fennel seeds

small red chilli (optional)

½ tsp unsalted butter,
softened

cinnamon stick for
garnish

Add the apple juice, lemon juice, orange juice, zests, spices and fennel seeds to a pan. Simmer over a medium heat for 20 minutes but do not allow to boil. If you're adding chilli, do so halfway through and keep tasting. Remove if it starts to become too spicy. The idea is to add a little gentle background heat that is barely noticeable.

Ladle the liquid into a heatproof glass or mug, leaving the zest and spices in the pan if you wish. Add about half a teaspoon of butter to your glass. Serve with a cinnamon stick to garnish.

INSPIRATION I've had many versions of hot apple or cider over the years, but this is one of my favourites. It's incredibly warming at the end of a long walk or on arriving home after a cold, busy day.

FLAVOUR It might sound odd to use butter in a drink, but it adds a lovely savoury depth. You can also play with the flavours a little – add citrus zest or a pinch of ground cinnamon to your softened butter, or add a dash of maple syrup if your apples are a little tart.

Thai Coconut Tea

FOR 2

You will need:
2 tall heatproof glasses

500ml water

2 black tea bags

45g granulated sugar

2 star anise

1 green cardamom pod, smashed

2 whole cloves

½ vanilla pod, split in half, or ¼ tsp vanilla extract

3 tbsp coconut milk

2 lemongrass stalks to stir

Bring a pan containing 500ml of water to the boil and add the tea bags, sugar, star anise, cardamom pod and whole cloves. Stir the ingredients together until all of the sugar has dissolved.

Boil for a further 3 minutes, then remove from the heat and add the vanilla pod or extract. Allow the tea to steep for at least 30 minutes, preferably an hour.

Remove the tea bags and spices and discard. Reheat the liquid gently, then divide between two heatproof glasses. Spoon the coconut milk on top – if the milk is very thick, whisk in a little normal milk or coconut water until it's easy to pour. Add a stalk of lemongrass to each glass to stir.

ADAPT This will keep happily in the fridge for a few days without the milk, so it might be worth making a larger volume and saving some for later. It also tastes fantastic chilled. Just fill your glasses with ice, pour in the cold tea and float the coconut milk on top.

Smoke and Ruby Tumbler

. . . .

FOR 1

You will need:
tumbler

120ml freshly squeezed ruby grapefruit juice

ice cubes

20ml Smoky Lapsang Syrup (see page 23)

a good squeeze of lemon juice

a strip of grapefruit peel to garnish

Pour the grapefruit juice over ice in a small tumbler and then add the syrup to taste. You're aiming for a sweet, smoky background to the brighter, citrusy grapefruit. Add a good squeeze of lemon juice and stir. Garnish with a strip of grapefruit peel.

FLAVOUR Lapsang syrup provides a hint of the smoky, caramel taste of a Highland single malt whisky. When partnered with tart grapefruit, it's delicious to drink by a bonfire when your cheeks are hot and your feet are cold.

Pear and Rosemary on the Rocks

FOR 1

You will need:
tumbler, shaker, strainer

60ml pear juice from 2 small pears, or good-quality shop-bought pear juice (not from concentrate)

30ml freshly squeezed lemon juice

25ml Simple Herb Syrup made with rosemary (see page 22)

ice cubes

sparkling water

a sprig of rosemary and a slice of pear to garnish

Combine the pear juice, lemon juice and rosemary syrup in a cocktail shaker with ice, and shake well. Strain into a rocks glass and top with a splash of sparkling water.

Garnish with a sprig of rosemary and a slice of pear. For a longer drink, add more water and a dash of lemonade.

FLAVOUR This is an elegant drink for an autumn evening, as the shadows begin to lengthen and a chill appears in the air. For me, a ripe pear is a luscious and fragrant treat, particularly when paired with a hint of warm, woody rosemary.

Earl Grey Hot Toddy

FOR 1

You will need:
heatproof glass or mug

1 Earl Grey tea bag

a sprig of lemon thyme

235ml boiling water

2 tbsp freshly squeezed lemon juice

honey

a thin slice of lemon to garnish

Place the tea bag and lemon thyme in a heatproof glass or mug. Cover them with boiling water and steep for 4 minutes.

Remove the tea bag without pressing on it, then add the lemon juice. Stir gently and add honey to taste. Garnish with a thin slice of lemon.

FLAVOUR A hot toddy is a must for chilly days. Earl Grey brings with it a hint of bergamot, which, when paired with aromatic lemon thyme, makes everything feel fresh and bright. This is perfect for thawing frozen fingers.

FIRESIDE GLOW

As the cold weather begins to creep in, a crackling fire and drinks to sip with family and friends are essential. When you're snuggled up at home, these drinks will warm your taste buds and your spirit.

Blackberry Seedlip Smash

. . . .

FOR 1

You will need:
tumbler, muddler

5 large blackberries

½ a lime

1 tbsp sugar

crushed ice

30ml Seedlip Spice 94

sparkling water

a wedge of lime to
garnish

Muddle the blackberries with the lime
and sugar in your tumbler. Partially
fill the glass with crushed ice, add the
Seedlip and top up with sparkling water.
Serve with a wedge of lime.

INSPIRATION The thrill of heading
home from blackberry-picking with a bag
full of dark juicy fruit never disappears.
Jake, my lurcher, stands resignedly as I
promise, 'Just that last bush, then we'll
go home.' Your fingers may be scratched
and stained but the bounty is worth it.

After Eight Martini

FOR 1

You will need:
*chilled Martini glass,
shaker*

1 tbsp chocolate ganache
(see recipe below)

50ml double cream

30ml Simple Herb Syrup
made with mint (see
page 22)

ice cubes

mint leaf or sprig to
garnish

Put a tablespoon of ganache into a pan
with the cream and mint syrup, and heat
very gently until the ingredients are
blended. Allow the mixture to cool, then
pour into a shaker with some cubes of
ice, and shake.

Working quickly, pour the drink into a
chilled Martini glass and garnish with a
sprig or leaf of mint.

INSPIRATION This is a real after-dinner
treat, rich and chocolatey with a hint of
mint. I remember stealing After Eight
chocolates from my grandparents as a
child, and feeling deliciously wicked
while licking sticky fingers.

For the chocolate ganache

235ml double cream

250g good-quality dark
chocolate, grated

Put the cream in a pan and heat gently.
Bring just to the point of boiling and keep
watch to stop it from boiling over. Add the
grated chocolate and whisk until smooth.

Transfer to a sterilized container and
store in the fridge. It will keep happily for
up to a month, but keep it well covered so
it doesn't absorb any fridge flavours.

It doesn't take long to make and is also
delicious whisked into a cup of hot milk
on a cold, grey afternoon.

Fragrant Tea Flower Punch

FOR 2

You will need:
*punchbowl or heatproof
jug or jar, and
2 heatproof glasses*

100ml freshly squeezed
lemon juice

250ml clear or cloudy
apple juice

1 flowering jasmine
tea bud

600ml boiling water

100ml Spice Syrup
(see page 24)

2 thin slices of lemon
to garnish

Put the lemon juice and apple juice in a pan. Warm gently but don't allow to boil.

Place the tea bud in a heatproof punchbowl and add the 600ml of boiling water. After a few minutes, once the tea bud has unfurled, add the spice syrup and warmed fruit juices. Taste and add more syrup or lemon if needed.

Serve in heatproof glasses with a thin slice of lemon to garnish.

FLAVOUR This is a light and fruity yet warm and spicy punch with the wonderful scent of a tea flower. And there's something very exotic about bringing a fragrant bowl of punch to share between friends.

Vanilla Cranberry Cocktail

FOR 1

You will need:
chilled coupette or Martini glass, shaker

½ tsp finely grated orange zest

½ tsp finely grated lime zest

½ tbsp freshly squeezed lime juice

100ml cranberry juice

1 scoop good-quality vanilla ice-cream

3–5 fresh or frozen cranberries or autumn raspberries

Combine the orange and lime zests, lime juice, cranberry juice and vanilla ice-cream in a shaker, and shake vigorously. Pour into a chilled glass and allow to stand for a few seconds so that the foam settles. Decorate with fresh or frozen cranberries or raspberries.

FLAVOUR A fireside treat, this cocktail reminds me of winter sunsets. It's a fruity, creamy, not-too-sweet pudding in a glass.

Espresso Mint Martini

. . . .

FOR 1

You will need:
*chilled Martini glass,
shaker*

100ml espresso

ice cubes

25ml Simple Herb Syrup
made with mint (see
page 22)

Make a strong espresso and allow to cool
before pouring over ice cubes in a shaker.
Working quickly, add the mint syrup
and shake vigorously. The faster your
shaking, the greater the chance of getting
a lovely espresso head of foam. Pour into
a chilled Martini glass.

ADAPT There's something very grown-
up about an espresso Martini, and this is
a great after-dinner fireside drink, with
just a hint of mint. I sometimes like to
add a few drops of almond extract and a
splash of sugar syrup in place of the mint
syrup. If it's late at night, this Martini
is just as delicious made with decaf
espresso.

Mexican Chilli Cacao

. . . .

FOR 1

You will need:
heatproof bowl and glass

1 cinnamon stick

½ an ancho chilli

150ml milk of your choice

50g good-quality dark chocolate, chopped or finely grated

1 tsp light muscovado sugar

a pinch of sea salt

dark chocolate shavings for garnish

cinnamon stick to stir

Add the cinnamon stick and the ancho chilli to the milk and simmer over a low heat until fragrant, which will probably take around about 5–10 minutes.

Add the chopped chocolate to a heatproof bowl. Remove the cinnamon stick and the ancho chilli from the hot milk, add the sugar and a pinch of salt, and pour the milk over the chocolate. Whisk them together until they're thick and frothy. Serve immediately in a heatproof glass, garnished with chocolate shavings and a cinnamon stick.

FLAVOUR This is a real treat for when you're in need of a bit of nurturing. The ancho chilli adds a depth of flavour and mild, sweet heat to the warm chocolate. It's perfect for snuggling up with under a blanket on a chilly afternoon, or for sipping by a roaring bonfire.

Tamarind Spice Glow

. . . .

FOR 1

You will need:
heatproof glass or cup

1 tsp pure tamarind paste

1 tsp Spice Syrup
(see page 24)

300ml not quite boiling
water

2 thin slices of lemon

Add the tamarind paste and spice syrup to a heatproof glass or cup and mix together with a little hot water. Top up with the rest of the water and add a slice or two of lemon.

If you want to serve it chilled, pour the cooled liquid over a glass of crushed ice before you add the lemon slice.

FLAVOUR Tamarind paste comes from the fruit pods of tamarind trees found in Asia, and has a delicious sweet-tart taste. It's unique and hints at exotic places, marrying well with lightly spiced syrup to soften the sourness, and is full of antioxidants. The pods need to be soaked in water for about 15 minutes, then mashed and strained to extract the seeds and paste. The paste can be found ready-prepared in supermarkets but make sure it's pure tamarind and not a sauce.

Pomegranate Negroni

. . . .

FOR 1

You will need:
tumbler

200ml pomegranate juice

2 tsp Montmorency
cherry concentrate

ice cubes

3 good dashes of
Angostura Bitters

a twist of orange peel

Pour the pomegranate juice and cherry
concentrate into a glass of ice, then stir
well before shaking in the Angostura
Bitters. The drink should have a bitter-
sweet tang, so add more Angostura if
needed. Twist the orange peel on top of
the drink to release the oils.

FLAVOUR The cherry concentrate
gives an extra layer but isn't essential.
However, I recommend keeping the
cherry concentrate in the fridge as a
sugar-free cordial. It's also delicious with
hot water.

Index

Acknowledgements

Many thanks to my editor, Lizzy Goudsmit, and Susanna Wadeson for believing I could do this. A huge thank you to the wonderful team at The Talbot Inn for their help and encouragement, to the talented Jason Ingram for his photos and to Isobel Gillan for her design.

Thanks to my wonderful family for their constant love and encouragement, to Joanna Weinberg for all the tasting and creating we have done together, and to Jackie, Lou and Sarah for dog walks and sanity.

Finally, love and huge thanks to my wonderful Matt, Amelie and Rafael for all their tasting, comments, love, and for putting up with the mess.

TRANSWORLD PUBLISHERS
61–63 Uxbridge Road, London W5 5SA
www.penguin.co.uk

Transworld is part of the Penguin Random House group of companies whose addresses can be found at global.penguinrandomhouse.com

Penguin
Random House
UK

First published in Great Britain in 2017 by Bantam Press, an imprint of Transworld Publishers

Copyright © Transworld Publishers 2017

Recipes: Clare Liardet
Photography: Jason Ingram
Line illustrations: Beci Kelly
Design: Isobel Gillan

Clare Liardet has asserted her right under the Copyright, Designs and Patents Act 1988 to be identified as the author of this work.

A CIP catalogue record for this book is available from the British Library.

ISBN 9780593079454

Typeset in Ehrhardt and Archer
Printed in China

Penguin Random House is committed to a sustainable future for our business, our readers and our planet. This book is made from Forest Stewardship Council® certified paper.

1 3 5 7 9 10 8 6 4 2